FINDING THE WAY

ON THE CAMINO DE SANTIAGO

Ann Morrison

Copyright © 2017 Ann Morrison

Finding The Way on the Camino de Santiago

Published in 2017 by Flying Spoke Media

Boulder, Colorado, USA

All rights reserved. No part of this book may be reproduced, stored in a retrieval system or transmitted, in any form or by any means, without the prior written consent of the author.

Photographs contributed by people other than the author are not included in the copyright for this text. Third-party photographers retain all rights to their own work.

ISBN: 0998581402

ISBN-13: 978-0998581408

For more information, please contact ann@flyingspokemedia.com

CONTENTS

Preface	vii
Introduction	9
The Journey	15

    Why the Camino?
    Enjoy the journey
    Beware of others' stages
    Be aware of judgments
    Distances can be deceptive

Camigos	27

    Create a sense of belonging
    Reassure others
    Celebrate others
    Everyone has "something"

Baggage	37

    Possessions can be burdensome
    Emotions can be burdensome
    Phones can be burdensome
    My negative thoughts don't help me
    My decisions, my consequences

Goals and Expectations	49

    Expectations can change
    Periodically check progress toward goals
    It can be good to jump into things
    It can be good to work up to things

Faith and Control · 57

- Every day brings surprises
- I can't control everything
- God's got my back
- Listen carefully
- I am as God intends me
- Mistakes can be gifts
- Let others make mistakes

Challenges · 75

- I can change my thinking
- Put one foot in front of the other
- Welcome adversity as an opportunity
- Tread carefully in unpredictable terrain
- Difficult days allow sweet rewards

Health and Wellbeing · 89

- Rest intentionally
- Don't let things fester
- Make good choices with money
- Give aches and wounds time to heal
- I am responsible for my happiness
- Others are responsible for their happiness

Traveler as Guest · 99

- Be respectful of others' requests
- Not all thoughts need to be shared
- Learn others' languages
- Be polite
- Keep the peace
- Learn others' customs

Conclusion · 109

Photo Credits · 111

Opposite: St. Jean Pied de Port
Photo: Miguel Ángel García

Quiet Outside Triacastela   Photo: Author

Preface

The Camino de Santiago refers to dozens of pilgrimage routes that end in the town of Santiago de Compostela in northwest Spain.

The pilgrimage paths follow ancient Roman trade routes and the journeys were popular in the Middle Ages. For hundreds of years, people began the journey on foot or horseback from the front door of their homes all over Europe heading to the burial place of the remains of St. James.

Today some routes are more popular than others, the most traveled being the 500 miles from St. Jean Pied de Port, France to Santiago de Compostela, Spain. Pilgrims walk, ride bicycles or horses, or unicycles, as we saw one person do.

Pilgrims begin their journey from any of hundreds of towns along the pilgrimage routes, joining others who are already on their way to Santiago.

Pilgrims typically walk anywhere from four to twelve hours each day, spending time alone in thought as well as with fellow pilgrims from all over the world. The journey is filled with both pleasant surprises and painful challenges.

The ideas in this book are based on my pilgrimage from Ponferrada to Santiago de Compostela with my husband in May 2016.

Yellow arrows painted on signs, buildings, rocks, fences, and other structures direct pilgrims to Santiago. The arrows line many of the same paths traveled by pilgrims since the Middle Ages.

Mark and I took this trip to celebrate our 25th wedding anniversary and 50th birthdays. We married at age 25 and spent the subsequent 25 years raising two sons, earning graduate degrees, developing professional careers, and doing everything that went with those activities.

With our professional lives settled and our sons moved out of the house, life had quieted down. It was a good point in our lives to take a break for introspection.

Each day we walked I actively thought about the person I was and the person I aspired to be. I walked and thought, watched and listened. I questioned many things in my life, including my values.

Along the way I experienced events and interactions that personified the values and personal principles that were becoming clear to me as I disentangled and evaluated the events of the previous 25 years. Examples emerged in nature, architecture, those who lived along the Camino route, my fellow pilgrims, and myself.

I came to think of the values and personal principles like the yellow arrows that provided direction for us each day. The arrows guided us on our journey. When we weren't sure which way to go, we looked for an arrow. Like the yellow arrows, the ideas in these pages are my guides. They show me the way when I am not sure which way to turn.

These pages are a record of some of my guiding ideas and how I came to see them with more clarity while walking The Way of St. James. I hope that in sharing, and often laughing at my own thoughts and feelings, that others might be prompted to think about their own.

This book is not an effort to tell others how to live their lives. These guiding ideas are my own and readers may or may not share them. Each of us has our own set of guiding ideas which are, and should be, unique.

Further, every person's experience of pilgrimage is their own. One of the beauties of being human is that we each experience the world uniquely. This book is solely about my experience, one of the most powerful of my life.

I would like to acknowledge our Camigos Poul, Margit, Chris, Susan, Jan, Sheila, Matt, Debbie, Sigrun, and Gerd for sharing their Caminos with us.

Thank you to all of the brilliant photographers whose use of Creative Commons licensing allowed the inclusion of their beautiful images.

I am grateful to those whose teachings are woven throughout these pages: Rob and Chris Morrison, Joan and Hillary Don, Peggy McEachen, Chrissy Farwell, Kathleen Morrison, Suzanne Vallely, and Fr. Peter Mussett. I love you all.

To Mark, my most valued companion and traveling partner, and my ultimate blessing. You give me perspective and joy every day.

Ann Morrison
Boulder, Colorado

Introduction

My husband, Mark, and I went to Sunday Mass in Ponferrada the day before we left on our Camino. During Mass, I asked myself why I was on the Camino. While I didn't have an answer to that question, I did spend time thinking about a homily I once heard about being human. My understanding of the homily was that we are all human and that as humans we are all flawed and constantly making mistakes. Our job is to recognize and acknowledge our mistakes and try our best not to repeat them.

After Mass we went to a shop to purchase scallop shells that traditionally hang from backpacks, identifying the bearer as a Camino pilgrim. I had four to choose from. Three were perfect in shape and color.

The fourth shell had a noticeable chip in it (see photo on cover). While not ugly, it was not pretty like the others. From a distance, the chip wouldn't be noticeable. Up close, however, the chip was the first thing my eye was drawn to.

Scallop shells, like those shown above, hang from pilgrims' backpacks
Photo: José Antonio Gil Martínez

Having just spent time thinking about humanness, I chose the chipped shell. In that moment I felt it appropriate that my shell should be analogous to my human imperfections.

Within hours, however, I hated the shell.

That night I lay awake considering whether to buy another, a perfect and pretty shell. What would I do with the chipped shell, I wondered. Would I throw it away? That didn't feel right to me.

There wasn't an obvious place to attach the shell to my pack, so I tied it around a very short piece of webbing right next to a clip. I thought that perhaps the clip would sever the thin string and I would lose the shell. If that happened, more than likely someone else would pick it up and I wouldn't have thrown it away. I could buy a new, perfect shell without guilt. The decision as to whether to get a new shell would be made for me.

We left early the next morning, my chipped shell hanging from my backpack.

Periodically throughout the day I checked to see if it was still attached. Each time I was disappointed to see it there and then felt guilty about my disappointment.

While I knew it was unlikely that anyone would think twice about the imperfection in my shell, I was still self-conscious about it. Part of me wondered if anyone would look at my shell and wonder why I had chosen one that was chipped. From well behind me, I knew, the shell would look like any other. Once others got close, however, I worried that they would see the imperfection in my shell and judge it. Judge me.

At the end of that first day the delicate string was intact and the chipped shell remained tied, like an advertisement of my shortcomings, on my pack.

Having the shell tied to the clip had proven inconvenient as it got in the way each time I opened and closed my pack so on the second day I retied the shell to a loop under the top of my backpack. The tie was protected but the shell bounced around and easily could have caught on something and pulled off. I wasn't careful when I put my pack on the ground near chairs, rocks, and buildings.

At the end of the second day, however, the flawed shell remained.

As I walked behind fellow pilgrims, I looked at their shells. No one else's had a chip or imperfection. All I saw were perfect and pretty like those I had passed up.

I was certain that not a single one of my fellow pilgrims was obsessing about the appearance of their shell, so why was I?

The third day, warming up to the shell, I tucked it under a flap so it wouldn't tear off. I halfheartedly decided to stop finding ways to inadvertently lose the shell, and made a tentative commitment to trying to like it, despite its flaws.

On the fourth day, I had my first opportunity to buy another shell and it became evident that my tentative acceptance of the flawed one was fragile.

I decided that if I did get a new shell I could leave the chipped one with the rocks that are often left on trail markers.

With the possibility of getting a new one, I picked a shell out of a basket in a small shop. Rather than being perfect, it had a chip in the exact same place as mine. I laughed at the coincidence and picked another out of a different basket. It, too, had a chip in the same place as the previous. Beginning to be suspicious that God was watching me, I chose a third from under a pile of shells, so I couldn't see it before I pulled it out. Familiar with God's work, the chip on the bottom right-hand edge did not surprise me.

"I get it", I said out loud and put the third shell down. I reached down to my pack and found a way to securely tie my shell to make sure that it was protected, wouldn't fall off, and wouldn't break. Then I walked away.

The thin string never broke and my shell returned home with me.

Scallop shell imagery can be found in many places, such as on this door handle.

Photo: Fresco Tours

It struck me that humans, like my shell, can appear perfect from a distance. As we get to know people, however, we often find that those whose lives may seem ideal, aren't. The internal and external turmoil we each encounter are frequently similar to our own. It is only when we come to know others well that we can find solace in our frailty and companionship in our challenges.

I still don't love the way my shell looks, but I do like that it was the one that accompanied me on my journey. It is a constant reminder that I am human and thus, flawed. My flawed shell gives me permission to be imperfect. It reminds me that, as a human, the best I can do is to recognize and acknowledge my mistakes and try my hardest not to repeat them.

Ultimately, while I spent so much time trying to release the flawed shell so that I could replace it with a perfect one, it has released me from my obligation to be a perfect person.

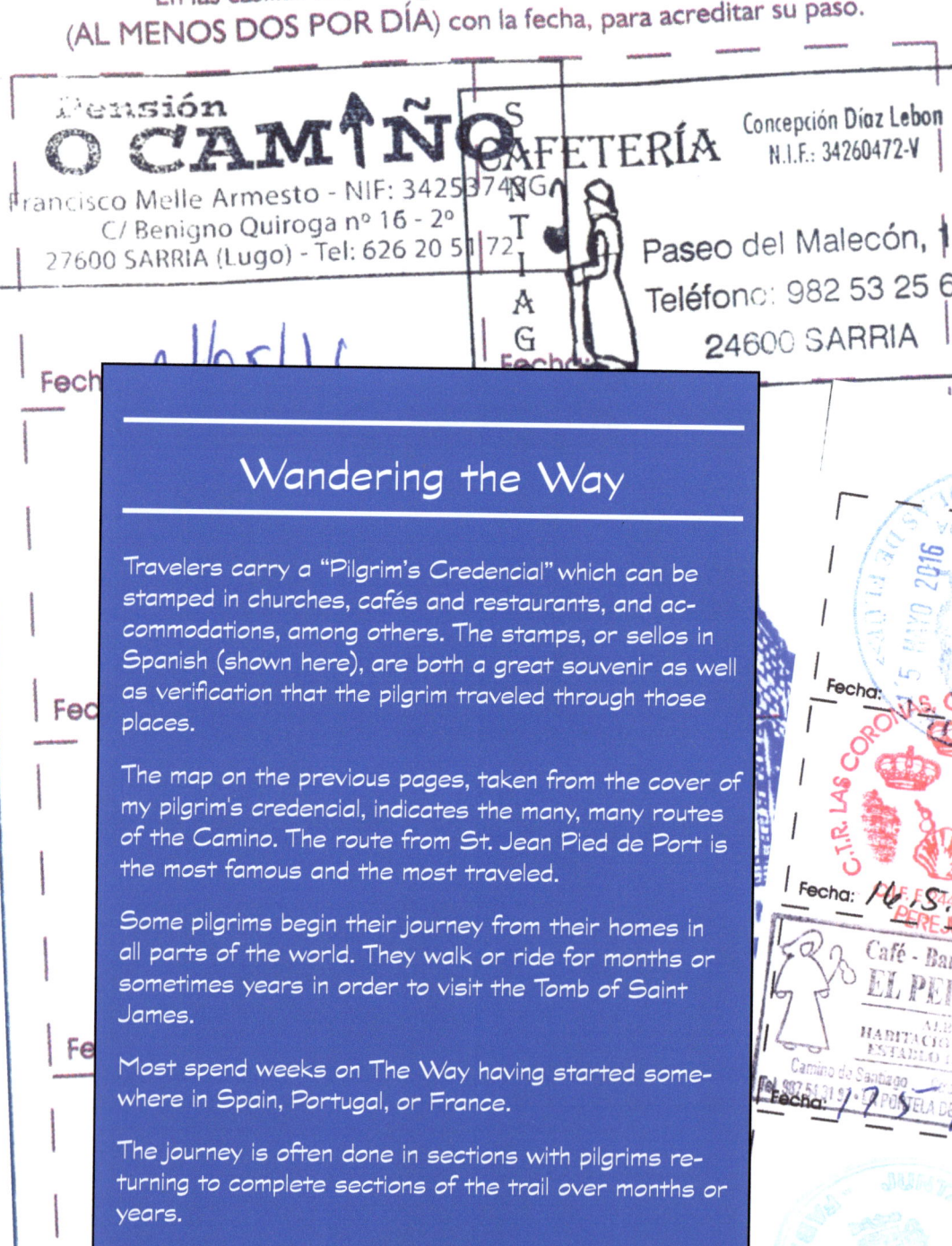

Wandering the Way

Travelers carry a "Pilgrim's Credencial" which can be stamped in churches, cafés and restaurants, and accommodations, among others. The stamps, or sellos in Spanish (shown here), are both a great souvenir as well as verification that the pilgrim traveled through those places.

The map on the previous pages, taken from the cover of my pilgrim's credential, indicates the many, many routes of the Camino. The route from St. Jean Pied de Port is the most famous and the most traveled.

Some pilgrims begin their journey from their homes in all parts of the world. They walk or ride for months or sometimes years in order to visit the Tomb of Saint James.

Most spend weeks on The Way having started somewhere in Spain, Portugal, or France.

The journey is often done in sections with pilgrims returning to complete sections of the trail over months or years.

The Journey

Why the Camino?

Walking the Camino is no ordinary vacation. It involves taking time from typical life to travel, but also involves exhaustion, physical pain, sleeping with strangers, snoring, oftentimes illness, and hours outdoors in unpredictable weather, among other things.

Those who choose the Camino are drawn to The Way for many reasons. Some seek healing. Others are drawn by the physical challenge. I had no such calling but hoped that I would find it along The Way.

When people asked me why I was on the Camino I had no better answer than: "to take time to think". My response seemed entirely acceptable. People were satisfied with it. That question always reminded me, however, that I didn't know why I was there.

> The best remedy for those who are afraid, lonely or unhappy is to go outside, somewhere where they can be quiet, alone with the heavens, nature and God. Because only then does one feel that all is as it should be.
>
> Anne Frank

I came to understand that I didn't need a reason. Although some people were very clear what drew them to the journey, it was okay that I wasn't.

I found that my lack of clarity about the purpose for my pilgrimage was beneficial in that I made it up as I went along. I had the time and space to consider a variety of possibilities that I wasn't able to think about in the context of my hectic daily life before I left for Spain.

Being open to thoughts about why I was on pilgrimage was also a key factor in allowing me to learn so much from so many. Because I didn't have a clear purpose in following The Way, I spent a lot of time wondering what I could learn from the experience.

Despite the challenges, and perhaps because of them, every day on the Camino is a gift.

Photos, left: people on path, Alex Bikfalvi; two women walking: Jose Antonio Gil Martinez; underwear: joan; bunk beds: Debbie Parsell; person in yellow poncho: Fresco Tours; medic: joan.

Enjoy the journey

The host at the Albergue in Ponferrada told us what he tells every pilgrim who is just starting their journey. He said that we aren't carrying a cross like Jesus and that intentional suffering was optional. He encouraged us to do what we needed to in order to enjoy our Camino. It was great advice.

The people we met, the beauty of the trail, and the daily physical activity all significantly contributed to our enjoyment.

> It is good to have an end to journey toward; but it is the journey that matters in the end.
> Ernest Hemingway

While we typically enjoyed each day, there were also times when we were too tired, wet, hot, aching, or generally uncomfortable to enjoy the journey.

It was then that I had to intentionally remind myself that every day on the Camino is a gift. Even in the midst of pain, fatigue, or discomfort, there was a multitude of reasons to enjoy every moment.

A hot day was a good reason to sit under a tree and listen to the birds. Hunger allowed me to look forward to a delicious meal and anticipate a refreshing lemon soda.

Every person I met had something to teach me. Every step I took was movement toward new understanding of myself, my life, and those I cared about.

Wandering the Way

Of pilgrims who completed the Camino in 2015, 38% indicated their motivations were religious, 8% cultural, and 54% said they traveled the Camino for both religious and cultural reasons.

Source: Oficina de Acogida al Peregrino

Each kilometer allowed the gift of a light heart and happiness, if I chose to enjoy the journey.

Opposite: The Rio Burbia is a serene setting in Villafranca del Bierzo.

Photo: Author

Beware of others' stages

Nearly all guidebooks separate parts of the routes into "stages" that equate, or are perceived as equating, to one days' walking.

Each of us has different preparation, physical stamina, emotional stamina, goals, etc., Because of this I think it is counterintuitive to imply that there are set stages or an expected way to make the pilgrimage.

Many people injure themselves because they have planned their trip based on prescribed stages without honoring their individual circumstances.

Preparation before embarking on the Camino is essential, but I believe that the wise pilgrim remembers that their journey should be dependent on our own circumstances, goals, and desires. A plan is only a plan and can be changed.

Wandering The Way

Many guide books and websites include a set of stages. Whether intentionally or not, these lists can be perceived as established stages or stages that most pilgrims use.

On The Way I heard a lot of frustration from pilgrims who, on their first Camino, followed what they perceived to be recommended stages.

There was common agreement that a greater emphasis on encouraging pilgrims to create their own stages based on their goals and fitness level would be beneficial. It is important for pilgrims to use the myriad of resources available in books and websites but also remain aware of options for accommodations in each town, however.

Camino Francés (French Way)
1. From St.-Jean-Pied-de-Port to Roncesvalles
2. From Roncesvalles to Larrasoaña
3. From Larrasoaña to Pamplona
4. From Pamplona to Puente la Reina
5. From Puente La Reina to Estella
6. From Estella to Torres del Rio
7. From Torres del Rio to Logroño
8. From Logroño to Nájera
9. From Nájera to Santo Domingo de la Calzada
10. From Santo Domingo de la Calzada to Belorado
11. From Belorado to San Juan de Ortega
12. From San Juan de Ortega to Burgos

Suggested stages, like the one above, are beneficial for planning the journey. Wise pilgrims remember that these are just ideas and that their own stages may differ significantly.

Be aware of judgments

Although we would like to think it doesn't happen, there is some amount of shaming on the Camino. Perceptions of a "right way" to travel the Camino can lead to judgment of those who do it differently. The phrase, "Everyone has their own Camino", is commonly heard in defense of people who are either judging others or judging themselves for not taking the Camino route as it somehow "should" be done.

The notion of how the Camino should be done inadvertently colored many of the conversations we had with fellow pilgrims.

Those who are walking sometimes think the bicyclists are taking the easy way. Riding in a taxi or bus can be perceived as weak. Stories of people who finish in record time, walking 40 or more kilometers per day, are laden with subtext of value and respect.

People walking with only day packs likely used the courier service that transports backpacks from one hotel to the next. It can be easy to think that "real" pilgrims carry all of their possessions with them each day.

Pilgrims on horses approaching El Cebreiro
Photo: Debbie Parsell

As a means of initiating conversation, it is common for people to ask others where they began the route. Mark and I began in Ponferrada, only 225 kilometers from Santiago. From the beginning, I didn't feel like we were doing enough. We could have started in Astorga but would have had several more long days, risking injury and not being able to finish or take time to enjoy the journey.

Before we left our priest reassured me that the distance we would travel was far less significant than how we would engage in the experience. Key to engagement was deep introspection and close and honest examination of what we found in our hearts. Our willingness to be transformed by the experience would define our pilgrimage, not the number of kilometers we walked.

I must have forgotten his wisdom early in the journey because every time someone asked me where we started I said that we had begun in Ponferrada and, without exception, qualified that we only had a limited amount of time off of work. The implication was that we would be as dedicated as anyone who had begun in St. Jean or beyond, if only we had enough time.

> Above all the grace and the gifts that Christ gives to his beloved is that of overcoming self.
> St. Francis of Assisi

Inevitably the other person would say, "Ah, everyone has their own Camino". I would nod and agree but didn't believe it. I did judge myself as less of a pilgrim than those who had started in St. Jean or beyond.

That changed when I turned judgment of myself to judgment of someone else. One day, while standing at a café waiting to order a drink, I met a man who was likewise waiting for a drink.

In the interest of passing time, I asked him where he started the Camino. "Sarria," he replied. There was a thick silence while I judged him. He was part of the enormous group of people who began in Sarria, the last major stop on the journey where someone could walk the minimum 100 kilometers required in order to receive a Compostela, the certificate verifying that the Camino had been completed. He quickly added that he and his wife were only able to get away from their jobs for a short time, the exact same qualification I had given since before we left home. Ironic.

Advertisements for taxis are strategically placed along The Way.
Photo: Author

Judgments are not necessarily bad. Evidence from research in psychology shows that our brains begin to form judgments before we are conscious of them. They are useful in that they allow us to evaluate our safety in the presence of others in our environment, and gauge our place in the context of a situation.

In the context of the Camino, however, judging others involves comparing our understanding of what it means to be a pilgrim, or how a pilgrimage should be done, to how others do it.

Although I would like to think of myself as not being a judgmental person, I found that it was easy for me to be judging, and I wasn't comfortable with it. I didn't like myself when I did it and it was counterproductive with becoming the person I want to be.

I think that the best I can do is to be consciously aware of my judgments and consider others' ideas and approaches with an open mind. To this end, I tried to stay aware of the negative judgments I made about others and made intentional efforts to consider others' approaches. At times I was successful, other times less so.

I reminded myself that I was doing a lot of things others could judge me for. When that didn't work, I remembered that I typically knew very little about my fellow pilgrims. Many may have debilitating tendinitis or painful sprains. Some have ailments. A walk that is easy for one person may be very difficult for another.

I considered the relationship between my judgment of others and how I judge myself. To what extent did I judge myself negatively? Did I feel like a "real" pilgrim or a fraud? If I could reduce negative judgments of myself, would forgiveness of others come more quickly?

I am certain that there is a link between the two so now I focus on being accepting of myself in hopes that I will be less inclined to judge others.

Distances can be deceptive

Inevitably, Mark and I would head out on a section of our daily journey and, at some point, ask each other how long it would be until the next stop. We would look at the map and have a discussion on whether we had already passed through this town or that. Many of the towns we encountered did not have signs that indicated the name of the town, which caused confusion. We would look at the elevation gains and losses and try to guess where we were. Electronic map apps helped get our bearings sometimes, but not always. Oftentimes we just kept walking, assuming the destination would become evident at some point.

Many factors influence recorded distances as well as perceptions of distances on the Camino.

Inconsistencies in maps can cause confusion. Some distances are measured point-to-point and others include variations from elevation gains and losses.

The exterior of our pilgrim's credencial included several maps of the various pilgrimage routes, including the two above.

Elevation gains and losses can be represented on different scales for various sections of the trail. Simply looking at the profile of an elevation doesn't provide enough information. A climb on one day may have been difficult. It can be easy to compare a future climb to the previous one in order to gauge its difficulty. Looking only at the profile of the elevation gains and losses is deceptive unless you take the scale of the elevation gain into account.

Measurements to the center of town or the town border will change the distance. The location of one's lodging relative to the map's measurement increases or decreases the distance on any given day.

Distances are rounded and the discarded remainders can add up. Pedometers and distance apps can have varying accuracy, making it difficult to gauge how far one has walked.

A fellow pilgrim may have walked a certain part of the trail one or more times before. Their memory of the walk will be influenced by their circumstances at the time. Walks in great weather can feel shorter than those in poor weather. Being tired, sick, or injured makes any day seem longer.

In the end, we decided that there was really no way to know exactly how far we had gone or how far we still had to go and that we would just keep walking. We remained confident that at some point we would get to a shower and a bed.

In many ways our ability to measure or predict the beginning and end of an experience, on the Camino or in our typical lives, can be difficult.

Wandering The Way

Upon completion of the journey, pilgrims can receive a Compostela, or a certificate of distance, or both. The Compostela indicates that the journey was done for religious or spiritual reasons.

In order to receive a Compostela in Santiago they must:

→ Have made the pilgrimage for religious or cultural reasons or with an "attitude of search".

→ Have traveled the 100 km on foot or horseback or the last 200 km by bicycle with an assumption that the pilgrim has begun their journey with the intention of visiting the Tomb of Saint James.

→ Have collected at least two stamps per day in the last 100 or 200 km respectively to verify their presence in those locations.

The certificate of distance indicates the place one began, starting and ending dates, and how many km were traveled.

Source: Oficina de Acogida al Peregrino

Left Some pilgrims pull their belongings on wheels. Photo: Author

Wandering the Way

Want to meet others before you head off?

The Camino de Santiago Forum is a great place to connect with other pilgrims who will be on The Way of Saint James at the same time you will.

Join the gang at https://www.caminodesantiago.me/community/

Top right: Ann and Mark, top left: Susan and Chris, middle left: Debbie, bottom left: Margit, Poul, and Mark

Camigos

Mark and I agreed that one of the most powerful gifts of our journey on the Camino was the friends, or Camigos, we made. Our Camigos were not only companions with whom to share a meal, laugh, drink, or experience, but people from whom we learned about the world, humanity, and ourselves.

> *Friendship is the source of the greatest pleasures, and without friends even the most agreeable pursuits become tedious.*
>
> *St. Thomas Aquinas*

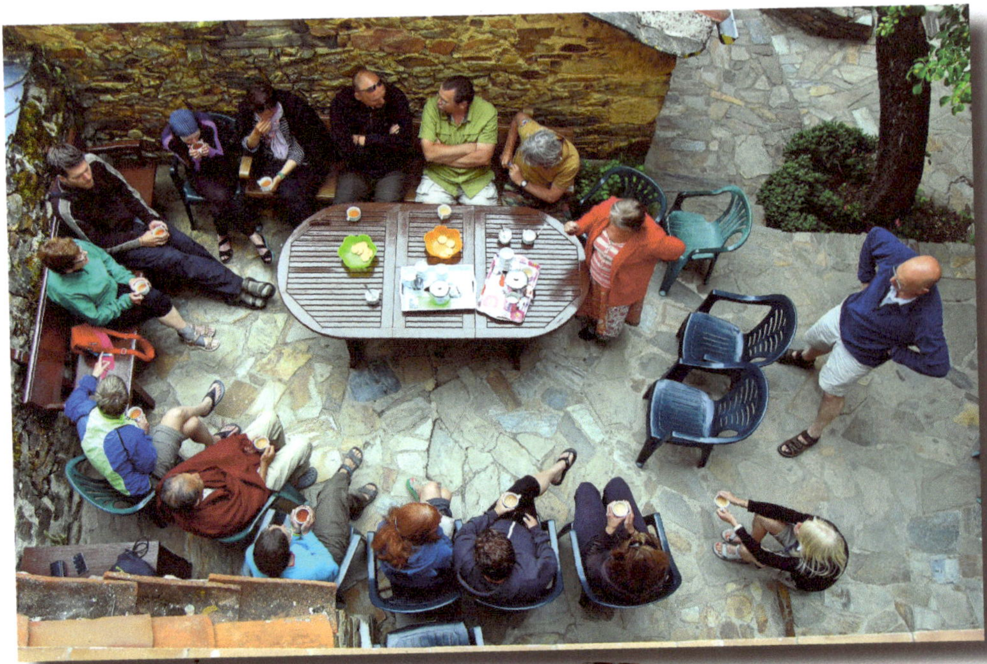

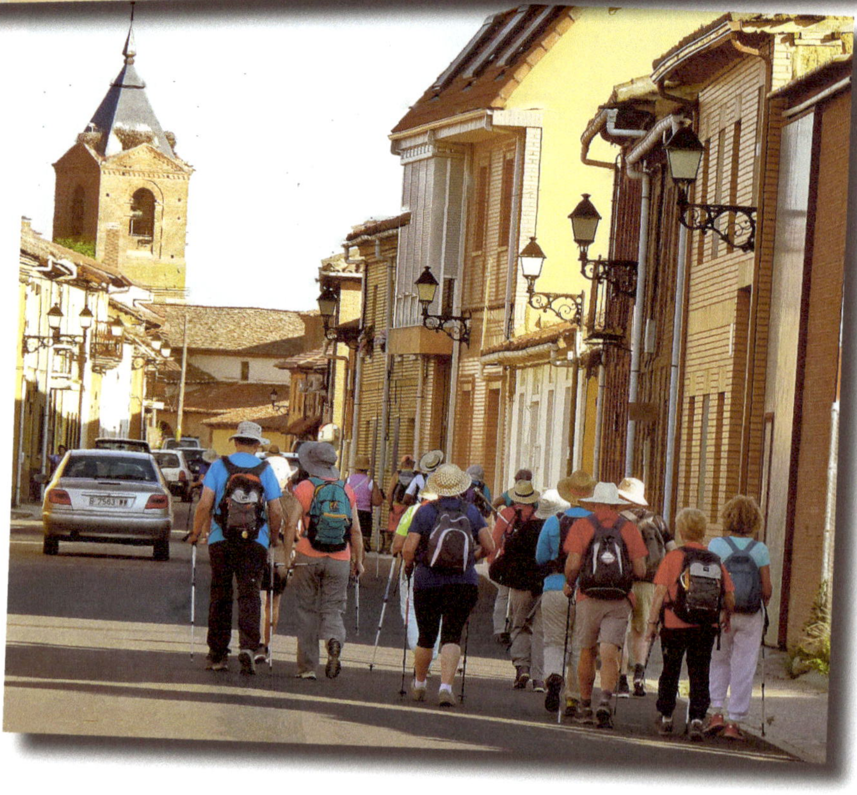

Create a sense of belonging

A great gift of Camigos is that they can provide a sense of belonging for others.

Daily, we looked forward to bumping into our Camigos at a café/bar along The Way. Mark and I would often approach a café/bar and find our Camigos already sitting there. They welcomed us with a boisterous greeting, as if it was a celebration that we had arrived to join in a rest and drink. We felt special and connected to the pilgrimage in a way that we wouldn't have otherwise.

During dinners, everyone related stories about the day's walk, laughing at the funny things we had seen. We lamented our aches, pains, and fatigue, and shared remedies. We looked at maps and discussed strategies for the next day's walk

Our Camigos had all begun their journeys in St. Jean Pied de Port. Rather than treating us like interlopers they welcomed us into their circle. In many ways, we didn't know what to expect and by sharing their experience our Camigos afforded us a sense of much-needed confidence.

Those who have experienced the Camino become a club of sorts. Many areas of the world have organizations for people who have traveled it or are planning their pilgrimage.

Familiar faces from the trail can be found throughout Santiago and beyond. I saw a young woman at the Madrid airport. She wore tights, trail shoes, and a t-shirt. She wrote in a journal and had a backpack at her feet. Dressed similarly, and carrying my backpack, she looked at me and I at her. Even without seeing her shell we knew that we had shared the pilgrim experience. We never spoke but as I walked by her, headed to my flight, we each raised a hand at the other in acknowledgment of our common bond.

> *Impart as much as you can of your spiritual being to those who are on the road with you, and accept as something precious what comes back to you from them.*
>
> Albert Schweitzer

Opposite page: There are many companies that offer group trips.
Photo, top: The Real McCoy; bottom: Instant 2010.

Photos: Dog: Marta Velasco; Roosters: Fresco Tours; Cow: Debbie Parsell; Snail: Fresco Tours; Horse: Fresco Tours

Confidants of the Camino

Walking alone provides time for thinking, talking to oneself, prayer.

Walking with others allows for conversation.

Sometimes, however, pilgrims may want to share thoughts and feelings, but not necessarily with another person. In this circumstance, there are a plethora of confidants who are guaranteed never to repeat your innermost secrets.

Pictured here are just a few of the confidants pilgrims may encounter.

Photos: Bull: BanxietyFree; Lamb: BanxietyFree; Pigs: joan; Ducks: Miran Rijavek

Reassure others

More often than not we were exhausted by the time we reached the place we were staying. We loathed the idea of walking another step to get dinner or go to the grocery or pharmacy. Because of our aches, pains, and fatigue, we missed many interesting features of most of the towns we stayed in.

Our Camigos, having traveled for weeks before we joined them, were much fitter than we were. Their blisters had come and gone. Their muscles knew what to expect and had given up complaining many kilometers earlier.

> Piglet sidled up to Pooh from behind.
> "Pooh!" he whispered.
> "Yes, Piglet?"
> "Nothing," said Piglet, taking Pooh's paw. "I just wanted to be sure of you."
> A.A. Milne, The House at Pooh Corner

As a result, our Camigos got to their lodging, took a shower and had a quick rest before they went out exploring. They had photos of things we hadn't seen and stories of interesting features of the towns where we had only slept.

I felt like a hack. I decided that we hadn't prepared well enough and felt bad about myself.

Upon expressing this one night, our Camigos assured us that they had felt the same in the first weeks of their journey. They recounted stories of blisters and falling asleep at 7:30 each evening.

I immediately felt better. I could be more accepting of and honest about my weariness. My self-doubt was alleviated in knowing that my fatigue was part of the pilgrim experience.

> ## Wandering the Way
>
> Some recent thread topics on the Camino de Santiago Forum include: "Doubts after day 1", "Is it worth it?", and "Everything is going wrong - help needed!"
>
> Responses from Forum members were heartwarming. with messages of encouragement and testimonials to having experienced similar circumstances.
>
> Find endless discussions on all things Camino related on the forum at caminodesantiago.me

Celebrate others

There is a multitude of achievements people accomplish along the Camino. Meeting goals both large and small. They wrestle with challenges, both physical and emotional, and are able to find a strength previously unknown to them.

Catedral de Leon
Photo: Jose Luis Cernadas Iglesias

These accomplishments are worth asking about, and they are worth celebrating. One such Camigo whose accomplishments were easy to celebrate was named Matt. Matt lost the lower portion of his leg to infection in 2006. Within a year of losing his leg, he walked the Camino. His prosthetic did not bend at the ankle. Despite this, he walked 500 miles from St. Jean Pied de Port to Santiago.

While on the trail Matt made friends with a woman from Luxembourg. They began walking together and on the downhill portions she walked forward and Matt walked backward with his hand on her shoulder. They made slow but steady progress and together they finished the long journey.

We met Matt on his second Camino pilgrimage. He told us that while completing the journey ten years earlier was an enormous achievement, he felt it was overshadowed by his need for assistance. This time he traveled alone, relying only on himself with the aid of a new prosthetic with a movable ankle.

I gained enormous respect for fellow pilgrims whose journeys marked significant personal breakthroughs, inspiring my own strength.

> *In everyone's life, at some time, our inner fire goes out. It is then burst into flame by an encounter with another human being. We should all be thankful for those people who rekindle the inner spirit.*
>
> *Albert Schweitzer*

Everyone has "something"

Think of a person you know who has the perfect life. They may be incredibly attractive, have an ideal body, be wealthy, have an exciting or glamorous job, a fabulous relationship, or any combination of those. At times I have felt envy toward those people.

Although they may seem to have a perfect life, they don't. In our interactions with acquaintances and co-workers, both in-person and on social media, we share only our accomplishments, which is appropriate in those contexts. This can lead others to believe the falsehood that everything in our lives is outstanding, which is never the case.

> *If envy was not such a tearing thing to feel it would be the most comic of sins. It is usually, if not always, based on a complete misunderstanding of another person's situation.*
> Monica Furlong

Although our public façade can appear blemish-free, each of us has experienced, is experiencing, or will experience humbling circumstances and events. One person may have emotional scars from growing up in a tumultuous household. Another may have lost a child or is living with financial insecurity.

Oftentimes, our day to day lives don't allow us time to listen and get to know others beyond the public persona they provide. Walking together, eating together, day in and day out over days or weeks provides opportunity to know our Camigos well. Learning about others' lives gives perspective to our own.

Conversations with pilgrims one has just met can begin with any of a number of ice-breakers such as "Where are you from?" or "Where did you start the Camino?"

> *There is no man in the world without some troubles or affliction, though he be a king or a pope.*
> Thomas á Kempis

If the product of those conversations invites further interaction, the pair might move into discussions about employment, family, favorite stops on the Camino, or other travel.

Once those topics have been exhausted the interaction can plateau with more mundane conversation that offers a multitude of directions. The benefits of seasoning chicken thighs versus marinating, whether the colors pink and orange clash or complement one another, or the relative contributions of the Beatles to the Rolling Stones to the evolution of music are all examples.

If trust has been established and interest remains it can be appropriate to share more personal challenges, usually in the context of life circumstances. This is when one may volunteer that although they touted the benefits of childlessness earlier in the conversation, the pain of four rounds of unsuccessful in-vitro fertilization cannot be mitigated by any amount of independence allowed by being unencumbered by children.

Path outside Triacastela
Photo: adrigu

Another pilgrim could share the self-doubt and financial strain resulting from three years of job searching after being downsized during the great recession.*

Those discussions are an opportunity to listen and ask non-judgmental questions, the things a good Camigo will do.

Knowledge of these challenges brings pilgrims together. Exposing our vulnerabilities with another person binds us in our human experience. Each of us has "something" that is the source of pain, misgivings, and doubts as they are essential elements of being human.

All examples are fictional.

St. Jean Pied de Port
Photo: Miguel Ángel García

Baggage

In this context, baggage refers to both physical possessions as well as emotional burdens. Both are relevant on the Camino.

Pilgrims carry all or some of their belongings while walking. The term "Every ounce counts" becomes very real at the end of a long day.

The Camino supports us in taking inventory of both our tangible and intangible baggage. What physical possessions do we own? What emotional weight do we carry?

Answers to these questions allow us to evaluate the extent we feel burdened by our possessions, our thoughts, and our feelings. Does our baggage drain energy, financial resources, and time that we would rather allocate elsewhere?

We can choose what baggage to continue carrying and which we need to release in order to live a more joyful life.

Photo: Miguel Ángel García

Possessions can be burdensome

I am sitting at dinner with Camigos from Delaware and Copenhagen, freezing in shorts and a sleeveless cotton shirt. My rain jacket is cold on my arms, not warm and cozy. Instead of enjoying a nice meal after a long walk I only want to return to my hotel room and climb into my warm sleeping bag. I wish I had brought my comfortable jeans, but I didn't because they are cotton, and every blog recommended leaving cotton at home.

Weather is variable on the Camino. Each of the routes stretch through differing climates, elevations, and terrain. Natural variations in weather add to the unpredictability of what clothing, equipment, footwear, medical, and first aid supplies one will need.

Equally, being on the road for multiple weeks or months can be stressful and many pilgrims may want at least a few of the comforts from home. Our Camigo, Poul, brought his own pillow. He was able to roll it up and it fit neatly into his pack. The weight and space it required was worth the comfort he received from it each night.

Carrying enough for every eventuality means a heavy backpack which is a greater burden on feet, ankles, and back. This results in greater fatigue and increased possibility of injury.

Carrying less allows for a lighter pack but might mean that you won't have a particular possession when you wish you did. You might find yourself uncomfortable because you don't have the heavy pants on a cold night or shorts on a hot afternoon.

Some packs are larger than others. An aside: the woman on the right is walking barefoot.
Photo: Debbie Parsell

Being limited to what you can carry on your back makes you more critical of what gets included. Needing to shed a pound forces you to set priorities and distinguish between the words "need" and "want."

Just two kilometers into our first day we realized that our packs were too heavy. A pair of new running shoes that had not been broken in were the first to go. I left them on the path, hoping they would be used by someone else. Mark put a pair of jeans in a nearby trash can.

Periodic chilliness aside, it was liberating to find how little I needed. Carrying everything on my back gave me a sense of self-reliance which became an important part of my journey.

The sun had barely risen on the first day of our journey before I lightened my backpack by leaving a pair of running shoes and small bag behind. Before we left my friend had said that I wouldn't need two pairs of walking shoes, but I wasn't sure. I could have sent them home from a post office, but chose to leave them for another pilgrim instead.

Photo: Author

Wandering the Way

Do you want to travel after finishing the Camino and will want additional or different clothing? Casaivar will hold packages for you. Send them from home and Ivar will hold them for you to pick up in Santiago. Find more information at http://www.casaivar.com/luggage-storage-in-santiago-de-compostela/

Wondering what to pack? There is an abundance of recommended packing lists on the internet. My two cents...if you wonder if you'll want or need it, take it and be ready to part with it if you find that the burden of carrying it outweighs the benefit it provides, you can either leave it behind or send it home.

Also, I wouldn't recommend bringing anything that would be difficult to replace. There are many opportunities for posessions to be left behind, stolen, or damaged.

Emotions can be burdensome

Like physical baggage, many pilgrims carry emotional baggage on the Camino in the form of misgivings, regrets, worries, questions, anger, or sorrow.

While often necessary, these feeling can weigh us down. Their burden can result in a significant tax on both our emotional and physical energy.

After decades of working, going to school, and being a wife and mother my emotional baggage had accumulated. As I walked I took stock of each thing that I was bothered by and evaluated whether I should keep it in my heart or let it go.

Finisterre. Photo: Miriam Mezzera

I realized that just as my backpack had limited space for clothing, toiletries, and first aid supplies, my heart had limited space for misgivings, regrets, and the like before it became too heavy and undermined my ability to make myself and those around me happy.

I decided to only continue to carry those feelings that were of utmost importance. Feelings that I decided were worthwhile of taking space in my heart were those that, while challenging, also provided guidance by reminding me of important lessons. Each one that remained served a purpose in contributing to becoming the person I want to be.

In discarding many of my misgivings, worries, regrets, anger, and sorrow, my heart began to float. I felt both emotionally and physically lighter. My mood lightened, my feet glided rather than clomped (at the beginning of the day anyway), and I could give love and forgiveness more readily.

Some of the emotional baggage I left along The Way were concerns I had for others. In assessing whether these concerns were productive, I questioned whether my concerns were helping those people. In a moment of brutal self-reflection and honesty, I realized that in some cases my concern was born out of a need for control as much as care.

> *Those who face that which is actually before them, unburdened by the past, undistracted by the future, these are they who live, who make the best use of their lives; these are those who have found the secret of contentment.*
>
> *Alban Goodier*

I decided that unless my concern for others' circumstances would result in my taking action that would aid them in a way they would welcome, others' concerns were their own. My job was to listen and be supportive when I could, but it was a tremendous relief to leave others' worries on the trail with my own.

Phones can be burdensome

Another aspect of burden I considered was the use of mobile phones. Phones serve many, many purposes on the Camino. They are cameras and often used to share the experience with friends and family at home through social media. They are also integral to meeting up with Camigos from town to town. We used our phone to contact the places we were going to stay, and when it was getting late and we hadn't arrived, they contacted us to confirm we were still on our way.

The downside of phones, in my view, is that they are also connections to our typical lives and can undermine our ability to detach from those things that we want to examine from afar. Technology that keeps us tethered can be both a convenience and an encumbrance.

My negative thoughts don't help me

Brutal honesty time...

On more than one occasion I fantasized about cyclists flying head over handlebars and landing in the mud.

It isn't pretty, but it is true.

Most bicyclists on the Camino were very respectful, riding on the paved roads when they were available and leaving dirt, rock, and gravel paths to the walkers. The respectful cyclists, when sharing the path with walkers, approached slowly and called out to make themselves known as a means of passing safely.

A few, however, yelled for walkers to get out of the way and then sped by. It seemed common for these same riders to yell "Buen Camino" as they raced by, seemingly as some attempt to mitigate their obnoxiousness.

At these times the peace I craved was disrupted. The quiet was crushed by the fun of a mountain bike race through a parade of pedestrians.

I ruminated with frustration. In my distress with these cyclists, I pictured what would happen if a lead rider of one of the groups happened to lose control of his bike. In my imagination, a cyclist at the front of one of the offending groups would lose traction on a rock and slow to try to regain control of his bike. In slowing, his friends, who would be following close and fast behind him, would lose control of their bikes as well. They would bump and skid, ending in a pile of bodies and bikes.

I would never actually want this mayhem to occur, but the fact that I felt the degree of frustration that led me to this vivid visualization was problematic.

After carrying feelings of frustration and the related visual images with me for several hours, rude bicyclists continued to race by, having the time of their lives.

I, however, lost half a day to brooding. On this beautiful day, when I should have been filled with joy, I chose anger. I realized this as I watched the back end of a cyclist disappear into a beautiful wooded grove, whooping with delight. He was thrilled and I was cranky. What was wrong here?

> I feel that we too often focus only on the negative aspects of life - on what is bad. If we were more willing to see the good and the beautiful things that surround us, we would be able to transform our families. From there, we would change our next-door neighbors and then others who live in our neighborhood or city. We would be able to bring peace and love to our world, which hungers so much for these things.
>
> Mother Teresa

My anger didn't impact the cyclists, it only impacted me. It disrupted the serenity I felt otherwise. This experience led me to question whether I was a good person. I felt bad about myself and realized that my thoughts served no purpose. They didn't result in the bicyclists changing their behavior. They didn't result in my feeling better. It was my choice whether to take control of my feelings or continue to allow them to control me. My negative thoughts were only hurting myself and those around me.

Photo, opposite: Antonio Lana Diazde Espada

My decisions, my consequences

Cookies have always been an important part of my life. Many of my life experiences have a cookie associated with them.

I ran the San Francisco Marathon when I was 18. I only trained for 6 weeks so naturally, I was taken to the first aid tent at the finish line. I don't know whether they considered it first aid, but I was given a cookie. That cookie did more for my recovery that day than any electrolytes could have.

Once, while on a hockey trip in Boston my son and I encountered a chocolate chip cookie that we dubbed "cookie of the world." For years, all subsequent chocolate chip cookies were measured against that one.

Santiago Tart is a specialty of the Galicia that dates back to the Middle Ages.
Photo: Debbie Parsell

Italian macaroons, Peak Freens chocolate crèmes, chewy molasses cookies, milk chocolate digestive biscuits, ginger snaps, and an almond macaroon sold by a small shopkeeper in Santiago are all among my favorites.

The cookie I will forever associate with the Camino is the Santiago Tart. To call Santiago Tart a cookie is a term of endearment for me, placing it in what I consider to be one of the higher forms of nutrition. Also, if you cut it smaller it could really pass for a bar cookie.

The Santiago Tart is the true utility player of cookies. It is a common dessert option because it is sweet. Protein from the almonds makes it a good breakfast. Because it is delicious it is also a nice treat in the afternoon. I am fairly certain that is has healing properties because my

Left: Pamplona
Photo: Miguel Ángel García

feet always felt better after sitting down to eat a piece in the middle of a walk.

I didn't do the Camino to lose weight but was getting substantial exercise every day. As such, I felt quite free to sample the cookies I encountered. I quickly found that the Lycra tights I wore each day grew more and more snug. My cookie consumption was exceeding my energy expenditure and instead of losing weight, I was gaining.

Rather than cut back on my cookies, I decided that the pleasure gained from sampling the cookies exceeded the discomfort of the increasing tightness of my clothes. That was my choice. I continued to intentionally seek out, discover, and sample new cookies. I loved both the hunt and the spoils.

The downside was that the carbohydrates and sugar made me feel sluggish. I walked more slowly and had a harder time jumping out of bed in the morning.

Consequences are a result of the things we do as well as the things we don't do.

Mark and I needed to travel from Santiago to Madrid to get our flight home. I hadn't worried about booking a train ticket as I had never had trouble traveling by train in Europe before.

Words to the wise: this highway sign means "turn your headlights on or you'll get a 100 Euro ticket".

The day before we were set to leave I looked online to see about buying a ticket, only to find that they were nearly all sold out. I tried to buy a ticket through the internet on my phone, but the system didn't work well and my purchase wouldn't go through.

Mark and I discussed going to the train station which was about a mile away, but it was raining and I was exhausted and we decided to get to the train station early the next day instead.

Tickets for the entire day were sold out when we arrived the next morning. We opted instead to rent a car and drive. It was more expensive, but we were pleased to have an alternative.

After 30 minutes in the rental car office, we headed back to the hotel to get our packs. We got lost and had an argument while trying to navigate a labyrinth of streets.

> Man must cease attributing his problems to his environment, and learn again to exercise his will - his personal responsibility in the realm of faith and morals.
> Albert Schweitzer

Once on our way we delighted in the scenery and reveled in our experience, until another car pulled in front of us and the driver put his arm out the window pointing his finger to the right. He wanted us to pull over to the shoulder. In response to our hesitation the driver turned on flashing red and blue lights in the rear window. We were getting pulled over by the highway patrol.

Evidently, the signs indicating that drivers should put their lights on in tunnels is a law rather than a suggestion. Furthermore, we learned one must possess an international driver's license to drive in Spain.

Who knew?!

After deliberation, the officers decided to drop the second charge, but in paying the first ticket our trip from Santiago to Madrid had already more than tripled.

We got lost between the hotel and the airport the next day, resulting in more tension and anxiety.

All of these stressful and costly experiences could have been avoided if we had braved the rain just one more time, knowing that the train tickets were nearly gone. We disregarded the signs indicating that headlights should be on in the tunnels. It wasn't the patrolmens' fault that we failed to do this, it was ours.

Just as I chose to continue to enjoy cookies of the Camino after I realized that they were adding pounds and made me feel sluggish, Mark and I chose to rest in our warm, dry apartment rather than brave the rain.

Just as the choices were ours, the consequences were too.

Photo: _The Real McCoy

Goals and Expectations

Different from a purpose, a goal is some outcome that a person hopes to achieve while on the Camino. There is something that the pilgrim expects will be different when they finish than when they began, and it is specific. They begin the Camino with some sense of what will make a successful journey.

What makes a "successful journey?" That is different for everyone, and many people begin without a goal at all. Short and long-term goals can emerge during the journey.

A plan to take each day as it comes, without goals, can be a goal in itself.

> ## Wandering the Way
>
> Want to get a sense of whether the Camino you have planned is reasonable for your interests and level of preparation? Ask questions and read what others have said on the topic on the Camino Forum,: https://www.caminodesantiago.me/community/

Expectations can change

By its very nature, the Camino is a dynamic, unpredictable experience which can make it difficult to set goals before beginning. There are often events that can impact pilgrims' plans in both minor and significant ways.

Some pilgrims have flexible schedules and the freedom to take the trip as it comes. Most, however, have scheduled travel or a need to be home that requires a timeline. Given that, most have planned which cities to get to by certain days. Illness and injury are common causes for having to modify schedules.

When someone gets ill or injured, it can be necessary to stay in one town for two or three days in order to rest and recover. Taking a bus or taxi can be required in order to get back on schedule which can, for some people, feel that their experience didn't meet their goal of walking the entire trail or that somehow they "cheated."

Every person I spoke with whose trips had been altered due to illness or injury expressed disappointment. Certainly, none of us sets off on the Camino with the intention of riding in a bus or taxi in place of walking.

Some pilgrims insist that they can "fight through", and do. Others compound their health problems in trying to "fight through" and fail to finish their pilgrimage at all. One woman fell severely ill upon landing in St. Jean Pied de Port, spent an entire week trying to get better, and then had to go home without ever beginning the physically demanding journey.

As I thought about this I wondered about the costs of modifying ones expectations versus the costs of holding on to them.

If one enters the experience without expectations or goals, do they have a yardstick by which to measure a successful journey? How does our anticipation of what may come evolve into expectations for what will come?

Before we left, I had researched the cultural and religious landmarks along, including Masses I wanted to attend. I envisioned us as both pilgrims and tourists with time and energy to visit significant points of interest after our daily walk.

Monastery of San Xulián de Samos; Photo: Author

To my significant disappointment, we visited very few of those places and only made it to a few Masses. Upon arriving at our lodging the last thing we wanted to do was put shoes back on and wander around town.

The most significant thing we missed was the opportunity to walk through the Holy Door at the Cathedral in Santiago de Compostela.

The Holy Door in the Basilica of St. Peter in Rome is typically covered with mortar and cement from the inside, effectively making a wall rather than a door. The Holy Door is opened during Jubilee years.

Pope Francis broke with tradition in deciding that the Holy Door would be open during 2016 to celebrate the Year of Mercy. He declared that "The Holy Door will become a Door of Mercy through which anyone who enters will experience the love of God who consoles, pardons, and instills hope."

By the time we arrived in Santiago we were exhausted. I had gotten ill the day before we arrived and Mark and I both needed rest.

The Holy Door closed in November 2016, and won't reopen until 2021. I felt sadness and regret all over again. I was upset with myself, thinking that if I had prepared better or been tougher or changed my priorities, we would have enjoyed this encounter.

Missing this experience, the Masses, and several other cultural and religious points of interest, doesn't mean that our journey was unsuccessful.

While developing my expectations for the trip before we left, I underestimated the physical requirements. Upon beginning, I realized that my expectations for the journey would have to change, and they did. We still had an incredible experience, but in different ways than we had anticipated when we planned the journey.

Puerta Santa de la Catedral de Santiago
Photo, Elanti

Above: an example of some of the whimsical structures along The Way.

Left: Santiago Tart and café con leche, a delicious breakfast, afternoon pick-me-up, or dessert.

Below: much of the religious imagery is interesting on multiple levels.

Photos: Author

Periodically check progress toward goals

There are many opportunities to slow progress along The Way. A common way is to take a wrong turn and inadvertently leave the trail.

Where a quiet, tree-lined trail departs onto a busy road, it can be easy to keep one's head down and continue on the more desirable, but wrong, route.

When this happens, pilgrims suspect they have walked away from the Camino route when they realize they haven't seen any of the guiding yellow arrows in some time. The absence of other pilgrims is another sign. In these situations pilgrims can backtrack, trying to remember where they might have gotten off track.

Many goals unrelated to the Camino journey also require that we check our progress. In order to reach them, it is necessary to stop occasionally to look backward, and then forward. Some course adjustment may be necessary.

As circumstances change it can be beneficial to evaluate the worthiness of a goal and consider changing it. Much of the wisdom about achieving goals in typical life assigns shame in revising goals, but I find that counterproductive. In my mind, meaningful goals are generated from knowledge of oneself that is, hopefully, continually evolving. Continuing to pursue goals that have become obsolete due to evolving circumstances can drain resources that should be allocated to moving in a positive direction.

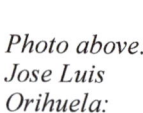

Photo above: Jose Luis Orihuela:

Photo, right: joan

Our Camigo, Chris, had a well-thought-out way of easing into his evening beer. He would begin with a non-alcoholic beer sometime in late morning, then move on to a lemon infused beer around noon. He continued with a shandy in mid-afternoon, had a real beer with dinner, and often finished with either a local wine or liqueur.

It can be good to work up to things

His daily progression provided some structure to his walk and gave him something to look forward to.

Our Camigo, Chris, enjoys a lemon-infused beer with his Spanish Omelette at lunch time. Photo: Author

It can be good to jump into things

Another man, a German, took the opposite approach. He began with beer at his first stop, had another at his second stop, and continued throughout the day. Beer was his water.

Whether you choose to build up to something or jump right in can be dependent on your goals, situation, and preferences. Both approaches, however, can be wonderful.

Catedral de Leon
Photo: Jose Luis Cernadas Iglesias

Faith and Control

The older I get the more I recognize those things that are out of my control. Rather than this realization making me nervous, a growing understanding that I don't need to control things because God is, gives me great peace.

I reexamined the blessings in my life as I walked, and I was overwhelmed by what felt like an abundance of riches.

I recognize great gifts in my life everyday. My husband and family, financial security, and health are all evident to me.

During our pilgrimage, I also examined the difficult parts of my life, times when I was significantly challenged, and how the lessons I learned from my shortcomings, mistakes, and significant weaknesses afforded me learning opportunities and subsequent wisdom.

> *When prayer removes distrust and doubt and enters the field of mental certainty, it becomes faith; and the universe is built on faith.*
>
> Ernest Holmes

All of this supported growth in my faith. I saw that God hasn't let me down yet. In second guessing Him I am not trusting, even though He has proven himself to me over and over again.

I find great peace in my faith that although I have to do my part, He has things under control and I can, and should, let go of worry.

Every day brings surprises

We can read the guidebooks, narratives, look at the maps, and talk to others who have done the Camino, but none of those things will show us the experience until we have journeyed it ourselves.

Guidebooks provide factual information about the journey. Maps give an idea of elevation changes, traditional and alternate routes, lodging, and meals. Narratives of others' experiences, including this one, are filtered based on the speaker's perspective.

> *God made the world round so we would never be able to see too far down the road.*
>
> Isak Dinesen

My adventures and surprises, both pleasant and distressing, will be different than yours.

Additionally, the way I encounter a circumstance is different than how someone else will encounter the same circumstance. Until I climb that hill, meet that person, or visit that town, I don't know what I will find.

Surprises can be the magic and become the substance of your memories. They are what make your Camino, "yours."

Opposite: O Cebreiro
Right: Albergue Casa Domingo, Palas de Rei
Photos: Author

Which way is The Way?

Photos, this page: top left: Fresco tours; middle right and middle left: Debbie Parsell; bottom right, joan; top right: Alberto Cabrera

Photos, opposite: top left, middle left, and bottom left: Fresco Tours; bottom right: Debbie Parsell

I can't control everything

> I believe God is managing affairs and that He doesn't need any advice from me. With God in charge, I believe everything will work out for the best in the end. So what is there to worry about.
>
> Henry Ford

Photo: _The Real McCoy

Things I can't control:

- The weather
- The deliciousness of Santiago Tart
- Whether or not a café will have Santiago Tart
- Hills and terrain on the trail
- Whether a washroom will have toilet paper
- Whether my laundry will dry before I have to wear it
- Bedbugs
- Sources of water
- When my next beer will arrive
- The music festival that plays until 5am
- People pooping near the trail
- Others' snoring
- My snoring
- Availability of hot water in the shower
- My husband hogging the blanket
- The number of people on the trail
- Inconsiderate bicyclists

Things I can control:

- Dressing properly
- Attending to my feet, legs, ankles, knees, and back
- Watching where I am walking
- My expectations
- Bringing my own food and drink
- Bringing my own toilet paper
- Using earplugs
- Having bedbug spray and a mattress cover
- Not looking at poop
- Leaving earlier or later each day
- Getting two pieces of Santiago Tart and keeping one in a baggie in my pack for when I have cravings
- Ordering two beers at a time
- My assumptions
- My paradigm
- Taking breaks
- Using sunscreen

God's got my back

This house appears to have two front doors. Unless it was plastered over, from the inside I imagine that the door on the third level looks a lot like that on the second level. From the inside, both could appear to be doors that one could open and go through.

Although we wouldn't be able to see this from inside the house, if we went through the door on the upper level, we would step onto the sloped overhang and possibly fall two stories down.

Going through the second level door, however, would lead us onto the safe platform and down the stairs, safely on our way.

From inside the house we wouldn't be able to tell which door is the right one, but God sees our situations from both inside and outside the house. Although it might not be immediately apparent, He leads us through the doors that are best for us.

Throughout my life there have been many possibilities that I thought were perfect but did not come to be. The house I loved on which the contract fell through or the ideal job that went to someone else are just two. At the time I was upset and didn't understand but in retrospect I am grateful.

I try to remember that God knows better than I do. He guides me to opportunities, both easy and difficult. I can't always see the wisdom in His choices right away but based on my past experiences I am confident that He's got my back and is looking out for me, even when I'm not.

> *Some of God's greatest gifts are unanswered prayers.*
>
> *Brooks, Alger, & Bastian*

Knowing that God's got my back allows me to free myself of my worries. When I trust Him I can let go of trying to control everything that happens in my life.

I still get anxious when I am waiting to see how a situation will work out or how circumstances which may not have been resolved as I had hoped were a manifestation of God having my best interest at heart.

As a flawed human, I need others looking out for me. I acknowledge that I can't do everything myself. I feel okay about that because in my core I know that God's got my back.

Opposite, Faith
Photo: Author

Listen carefully

It took time for me to hear myself and hear God on the Camino. In order to hear, I had to listen intentionally. Even with the abundance of time and space to think, it was easy to miss my thoughts and God's words if I wasn't being attentive.

Sometimes thoughts poured into my brain with the speed and power of a waterfall. I had to stop walking and write them down in order not lose them. It was as though an abundance of thoughts were flowing through a funnel and would become jammed if I didn't expel the current ones onto paper. Purging my thoughts in writing also gave me license to let go of old ones I didn't need anymore or didn't want to keep. Sometimes those thoughts had loitered in my mind for months, years, or even decades.

New thoughts were not necessarily the best or most considered. I found that thoughts from one day built upon those from the previous with evolving clarity and refinement.

Through thinking I was able to I untangle memories and emotions and make sense of them. Intentionally listening to myself and God was the beginning of that process.

> In vocal prayer we speak to God. In mental prayer He speaks to us. It is then that He pours Himself into us.
>
> Mother Teresa

Although my brain sometimes worked overtime to process my thinking, at other times I couldn't hear anything new or interesting. My brain was like an expansive desert, redundant and bland. I grew bored with myself and felt uninspired. I tried to watch and listen to see if anything would come, but often it didn't. Although I was often disappointed by this it made me appreciate those times of clarity all the more.

Photo: _The Real McCoy

I enjoyed stopping to write throughout the day.
Photo: Mark Morrison. Waiting for Ann.

I am as God intends me

Several years ago I complemented the hair of one of the university students at our parish. It was a set of shoulder length warm brown loose curls that framed her gentle, smiling face perfectly. In response to the compliment, she replied, "Thanks. God gave it to me."

That conversation prompted me to think differently about some of my characteristics. God gave me athletic calves that have run a marathon but don't fit easily into fashionable boots. He chose tighter brown curls that turn to frizz with just a whisper of the word "humidity." He gave me humor that is often entertaining but can also sometimes go awry.

As I walked I considered the things that I use to present myself to the world that compensate for, or even mask, some of my less desirable characteristics.

My makeup, how I dress, how I style my hair, the bags I use, the shoes I select, the car I drive, and the logos I display were all included.

As I made this list I wore no makeup, had crazy, curly "Camino hair", adorned no logos, was dressed in dirty tights and a smelly shirt. I wasn't driving my cool sports car nor was I sitting in my office with framed degrees on the wall behind me. Just looking at me you wouldn't know what schools I went to, what I do for a living, or where or how I live.

Without those things to moderate my interactions with others I was just me, the way God made me. My smile was the same. My heart was the same. My intellect was the same. Those were the things that people responded to. The impressions I gave others were dependent on who I was and how I felt about myself. I reasoned that if I was comfortable with myself, then others would be too. If they weren't, I decided, that would have to be okay.

It was uncomfortable at first. I felt frumpy. I was often smelly, dusty, frizzy, and sweaty. Even in this short time, my eyebrows grew to resemble caterpillars. My thick midsection bulged from under my t-shirt when I sat down.

One thing that made it easier was that there are fewer opportunities to look in a mirror on the Camino than in typical life. In addition, it was comforting that very few others made themselves up the way they would at home. Many people opted out of shaving or cutting their hair, including our Camigo, Poul, whose friends and family took to calling him "The pirate" upon seeing pictures of his beard and the relatively long, wavy hair under the buff he wore each day.

When I did look in a mirror I saw a pilgrim. Through my appearance I identified myself as a peregrino, one of the gang, so in retrospect, it wasn't any grand or brave experiment. The gift of the experience was that before long I began to feel the liberation of just being me.

I thought about characteristics of myself that I don't like as much as others and considered how they have been gifts. My athletic calves turn my bicycle wheels with power, my curly hair gives my stylist opportunity to demonstrate her skills, and I am the source of laughter much more often than I offend.

A beautiful day on the Camino with dirty tights, a smelly shirt, "Camino hair", and odds and ends hanging from my pack.

Photo: Mark Morrison. Walking with Ann.

I recalled the inspiration I found in the words of the university student who had attributed her pretty hair as a gift from God and decided that although I don't love it all, God made me the way he intended. Rather than disrespect His work, I should respond with a simple "thank you."

I will continue to drive my sportscar, wear my university sweatshirt, and style my hair, but now I still have confidence when I don't. I can choose these things because I like them, but as long as I remember that I am the way He intended, I don't need them. A tremendous liberation.

Mistakes can be gifts

On our first day on the Camino, we came to a fork where the trail split. A pilgrim standing at the intersection confidently told us that we could either continue to walk on a path adjacent to the road which would get us to our destination in 5 kilometers or split off onto a quiet road that wound through vineyards for 6 kilometers. Eager to get away from the busy road we opted for the longer, more pleasant route. We ignored the fact that most pilgrims chose to continue along the road.

Santiago de Compostela
Photo: Debbie Parsell

A short way along a farmer driving a tractor stopped us and said, "I am going to do you a big favor." He advised us to go back and take the road route. He said that the quiet, pretty route was much longer, more like 7 kilometers.

Mark and I agreed that we really didn't want to walk next to the road, ignored the farmer's wisdom, and continued through the vineyards.

The peaceful trail that initially provided us such joy soon became a nightmare. The road disappeared around corner after corner while hills appeared from nowhere. Cresting each hill we expected to see our destination only to find another hill. We were hot and exhausted. Our feet and backs ached.

At no point did we pull out a map, which would have been the sensible thing to do. We had relied solely on the knowledge of a fellow pilgrim and the advice of a local farmer.

> We don't receive wisdom; we must discover it for ourselves after a journey that no one can take for us or spare us.
>
> Marcel Proust

Although that day was painful, never again did we depend entirely on the knowledge or advice of others. We learned that in order to plan our day we had to reference not just one map, but several.

Photo: Miguel Ángel García

In order to make informed decisions about where to plan breaks, how much water we would need and what time we should leave in the morning, we had to use multiple sources.

If we had listened to the farmer's advice or followed the majority of our fellow pilgrims, we would have had a less painful day, but we wouldn't have learned this valuable lesson that provided great benefit for the rest of the trip.

The blessing of mistakes is that they afford us the opportunity to learn about the world and ourselves. Through them, we discover our own strengths and needs. We become more savvy to the world and gather learning that becomes wisdom.

Let others make mistakes

Oftentimes others benefit when we share our mistakes with them. Sentences that begin with, "Don't make the same mistake I did by..." can provide invaluable guidance.

Other times, however, others will only learn not to repeat the mistake if they make it themselves.

By preventing people from making less consequential mistakes, we are taking away their opportunity to learn about the world and themselves. Natural consequences can be the greatest teacher.

In addition, we cannot prevent another person from doing something that we anticipate will turn out badly. If someone knows that others have made a particular choice and deemed it a mistake, but make the same decision expecting a better result, that is their choice. We are not responsible for their choices. We can only provide guidance based on our own experience.

It is tempting to prevent others from doing things that we anticipate could be a mistake, but in doing so there are times we may be hurting, rather than helping them.

Common mistakes that pilgrims don't repeat:

→ Ignoring hot spots
→ Leaving too late in the morning
→ Skipping the sunscreen
→ Not bringing enough water
→ Leaving a charging cord or adapter in an albergue wall
→ Ignoring tendinitis
→ Leaving rain gear at home
→ Leaving a passport or money in a bag that is being transferred via courier
→ Buying new shoes the week before starting the journey

Opposite, Vidrieras de la Capilla de San Augustin, Roncesvalles

Photo: Miguel Ángel García

The climb to O Cebreiro affords expansive views
Photo: Author

CHALLENGES

The challenges we encounter in life are like friends who stop us and say, "Show me who you are."

> Character cannot be developed in ease and quiet. Only through experience of trial and suffering can the soul be strengthened, vision cleared, ambition inspired, and success achieved.
>
> Helen Adams Keller

I can change my thinking

Lots of pilgrims begin their journey in Sarria, which is 114 kilometers from Santiago. A pilgrim needs to walk a minimum of 100 km in order to receive a Compostela, the certificate verifying completion of the pilgrimage to Santiago de Compostela.

Until Sarria, our trip had been placid, tranquil. The volume of peregrinos appeared to expand three-hundred percent the morning we left Sarria, although statistics from the official pilgrims office in Santiago say that it is more like thirty percent.

Where previously people would pass one another with a quiet "Hola" or "Buen Camino", now no one bothered to acknowledge each other because the greetings would be constant. One woman who was trying to pass us in a narrow path yelled "Buen Camino", using the term more like a car's horn rather than a wish of goodwill.

> *The longest journey is the journey inward.*
> Dag Hammarkjold

The throngs of new people resulted in long lines for food, drink, and washrooms.

I struggled to be kind to the newcomers. As I explored why I felt challenged I realized that I felt that they had changed my Camino. Walking into Sarria we had passed a total of three people all day. There had been plenty of time for quiet reflection, prayer, and talking with Mark. I photographed the trail without having to wait for people to pass in order to get a picture without strangers in it.

After ruminating, I mentioned my frustrations to Mark. He said that he felt that more parade-like atmosphere made him think what of Mary, Joseph, and Jesus' pilgrimage to Jerusalem (Lk 2:44) must have been like. During their return from Jerusalem, Mary and Joseph found that Jesus wasn't in the caravan.

Mary and Joseph had walked an entire day before they realized that Jesus wasn't with them. Their pilgrimage route must have been swollen with people. Looking around, I reflected that Mary and Joseph would have thought that the volume of people in our caravan was light.

With Mark's perspective, I was able to change my thinking. It was easier to be kind and gracious to our new companions. Letting go of my frustration lightened my load. I was happier and continued the Camino as I chose.

While I can change my thinking, there are times that, for whatever reason, I don't.

As we reached Pedrouzo on the second to last day of the Camino I began to feel sick. By the time we got to our lodging I was miserable with a terrible cold.

The town was having a festival that evening. As we went to sleep that night a band began to play. The music was so loud that it sounded as though it was in the room next door. Even though I was exhausted, I had trouble sleeping. I laid awake, thinking that the music would end at midnight.

Midnight came and went, and the music continued. I thought it might end at 2 am, but 2 am came and went and the music continued. Three am came and went, as

The path can get very crowded as pilgrims near Santiago de Compostela
Photo: Instant 2010

did 4 am. At 5 am the band finished with, appropriately enough, Bon Jovi's *Living on a Prayer*.

The next morning we were anxious to get to Santiago and set off around 7:30 in the pouring rain. The rain continued all day, only letting up for about an hour. By the last few kilometers I was miserable. It was all I could do to put one foot in front of the other.

Just one kilometer away from our lodging in Santiago, we passed an elderly man walking down a steep hill as we walked up. He and I looked at each other and I silently expressed my pain. He must have understood me because he looked at Mark with sympathy.

In the midst of my misery, my wise husband, Mark, offered that the rain was kind of appropriate. He said that it was washing us of sin at the end of our journey.

At this, I coughed, blew my nose with wet Kleenex, and tucked my wet hands and sleeves under my rain poncho. I didn't use Mark's wisdom to adjust my perspective. I probably could have elaborated on Mark's thought, developing some positive perspective about the suffering of the pilgrimage, but I didn't. If I had, I probably would have been happier and more at peace but I didn't have the energy. I was wet, sick, exhausted, and miserable, and stayed that way until I got a shower, dinner, and bed.

In this experience, I realized that although I would have been happier if I had changed my thinking that day, it was okay that I didn't. Not changing my thinking didn't mean that I was a weak person, it meant that in that moment I felt weak. I was still a strong person in the midst of illness, fatigue, and exhaustion.

The Botafumeiro (shown right) in the Santiago de Compostela Cathedral is the largest censer, or incense burner, in the world. Eight tiraboleiros swing the Botafumeiro nearly to the roof of the transept of the Cathedral.

Photo, left: Debbie Parsell .

Photo, opposite: Daniel López García

Arrows indicating The Way come in various forms, such as this one outside Villafranca del Bierzo.

Photo: Author

Put one foot in front of the other

Sometimes when we are in a miserable situation there are no plausible options other than to endure it and continue to move forward.

Some days when we had miles to go, Mark and I wished we were done for the day. We were cold and wet or hot and sticky. Our feet or backs ached. We yearned for a shower, food, and bed.

In those times every step was effortful, sometimes painful. Not only did our bodies ache but our brains slowed. Simple problem-solving skills eluded us.

> By perseverance the snail reached the ark.
> Charles Haddon Spurgeon

When there were no other options and continuing to walk seemed impossible, we were still grateful for the certainty that every step was movement toward comfort.

Photo,: _The Real McCoy

Welcome adversity as an opportunity

Adversity tests us to become the best version of ourselves. Moments of adversity are an opportunity to discover strengths and gifts that we didn't previously know within us.

What does a pilgrim do when they lose their wallet, can't find a place to stay, or their only pair of shoes get soaked, but still have 12 miles to walk?

At these times we are pushed to come up with possibilities and options. Sometimes we may think that there are no options, in which case being innovative and thinking outside the box can be a strength we develop out of necessity.

> *The promised land always lies on the other side of a wilderness.*
> *Henry Havelock Ellis*

Without encountering these situations we may never have the opportunity to uncover our strength and ingenuity.

The benefit of facing and having overcome adversity is that we aren't as intimidated or scared the next time we encounter a seemingly insurmountable obstacle.

While it may seem even more daunting, facing adversity alone is an even greater gift. Opportunities to do things independently and either succeed or fail alone is how we become certain of ourselves and develop self-reliance and confidence in our personal strength.

Although difficult, encountering obstacles that force us to find the strengths within us can be a blessing.

Rainbow outside Pamplona. Rainbows are a product of rain.
Photo: Barney Schulte

Opposite: De Mansilla de las Mulas a León
Photo: Instant 2010

Terrain of the Trail

Photo, top left: Jose Antonio Gil Martinez; top right: Author

Photo bottom left: Debbie Parsell; bottom right: Author; opposite: BanxietyFree

Tread carefully in unpredictable terrain

The Camino is filled with hazards that can result in an early end to a joyous walk. A misstep on cobblestones or rocky paths can result in sprained ankles. Water from mud puddles can overflow into shoes, causing blisters. Stepping in cow poop is just plain gross.

As I scraped cow poop off of my shoe one day, I realized that the terrain of typical life can be just as unpredictable as that of the Camino. Situations at work or in our personal lives often need to be navigated with care. Oftentimes, circumstances involving unpredictable terrain are also high-stakes in that they can have significant implications for employment or relationships.

Difficult days allow sweet rewards

Lying in bed on a regular day feels really good. Lying in bed at the end of a long day on the Camino feels incredible. Food tastes better and drinks quench better after a difficult day than an easy one. Those satisfying tastes, quenching drinks, and welcome rests are only possible because of a difficult day.

Top, evidence of pilgrims enjoying themselves after a long day walking with Peregrina beer. Photo: Author

Bottom, a thick mattress is a welcome site to tired legs. Photo: Debbie Parsell

Top: chocolate and churros are a delicious combination in Santiago de Compostela photo: Debbie Parsell; left, Estrella Galicia is a favored beer. Photo: Manel; below: Fresco Tours.

Pulpo!

Pulpo, or octopus, is a delicacy of the region around Santiago.

Photos: Fresco Tours

Health and Wellbeing

It is important to stay healthy while on the Camino. It is common for pilgrims to fall ill and have to take several days to rest and recover. Sources of health care can be sporadic along The Way.

> *Be careful to preserve your health. It is a trick of the devil, which he employs to deceive good souls, to incite them to do more than they are able, in order that they may no longer be able to do anything.*
>
> St. Vincent de Paul

For this reason, eating well, drinking lots of water, resting, and attending to skin, muscle, and orthopedic issues are important.

Rest intentionally

Any single day on the Camino is manageable. The journey becomes difficult with the fatigue that accumulates from walking day after day.

The daily pilgrimage means that blisters grow wider and deeper; tendinitis and sprains swell larger and become disabling; and general fatigue yields to colds and flu.

We learned the benefit of planning rest stops from a Camigo - a good lesson. Each night Mark would look at the map for the next days' journey and plan our rest stops. We agreed to sit, have some food and drink, and take off our shoes and socks to let our feet dry approximately every 5 kilometers.

We knew what time we had to leave in the morning in order to get to the next stop in time for a shower, laundry, and a rest before dinner.

We also planned rest days where we spent two nights in the same place. We both slept in and took naps. We had time to let blisters dry out and visit the farmacia for supplies. Our muscles recovered and we did laundry. We stocked up on healthy food (and cookies). It was glorious.

Intentionally resting goes a long way toward reducing illness and injury. Sometimes slowing down means completing the journey instead of going home.

Left, Iglesia de Santiago, Boente, Spain
Photo: Author

Photo: Fresco Tours

Don't let things fester

Hot spots quickly become blisters. Tiny rocks in a shoe tear skin. Skin in damp socks folds over on itself, causing sores. Small aches develop into tendinitis. It is important to sit down and address these things right away.

Just as physical challenges can grow, so can social challenges. It can be difficult to spend day-in and day-out with the same person, even with the closest of friends or relatives.

Small frustrations can quickly become larger issues with traveling partners. The challenge in this, and the opportunity the challenge affords us, is to come up with ways to productively address tensions.

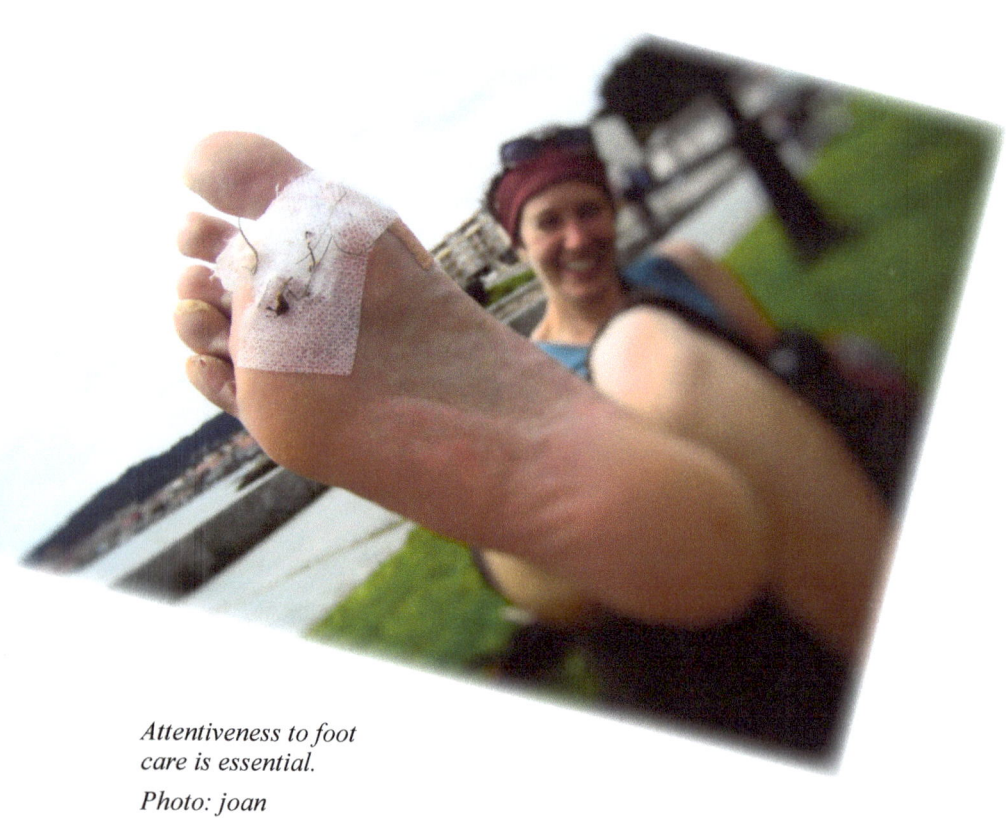

Attentiveness to foot care is essential.
Photo: joan

If I spend too much on cookies, then I won't have enough money for bedbug spray. It's just a fact.

Make good choices with money

Savings Time, photo: kozumel; Galleta Maria, photo: David Dennis

Opposite, De Mansilla de las Mulas a León, photo: Instant2010

Give aches and wounds time to heal

My fatigued legs ached after our daily walks. Even after a shower and a short nap, a flight of stairs could make my legs burn.

Most mornings my legs would feel refreshed as if they had fully recuperated overnight. Mark and I would compare how we felt and I would say that my legs were back to normal and that I felt great. It took only a short hill for my fatigue to return. I was reminded that many aches and wounds may seem healed but require more care, time, or rest for deep hurt to recuperate. Sprains, tendinitis, pulled muscles, and other aches and pains often take weeks or months to heal after finishing.

The same is true for personal aches and wounds. Given time and silence to think about life, it is inevitable that pilgrims revisit emotional hurt as well as joy. Walking and thinking can allow one to begin healing, but often recovery takes much longer. I have to believe, however, that investing energy in thinking about them can begin a healing process.

St. Jean Pied de Port
Photo: Miguel Ángel García

Photo, opposite: Instant2010

I am responsible for my happiness

After 25 years of marriage, my husband has not yet developed the idea to read my mind. If he were going to acquire this skill, I think he would have done it by now.

On one of our longer days we made the mistake of not leaving early enough. This meant that we were still walking into the late afternoon.

As we got closer to the end I sped up, anxious for a shower and to lie down. My husband remained at his pace and I found myself waiting for him at intervals. I snapped at him and he grew frustrated with me.

Photo: Author

Rather than getting snippy I should have identified some options and talked to him about them. I could have met him at the hotel. I could have used the time to take photos, write, or sit and have a drink. As it turned out I put my headphones on and listened to my audio book which took my mind off my exhaustion and helped me change my disposition.

It can be difficult to ask for things that will make us happy but then we can't complain if we aren't.

Just as I am in charge of my happiness, others' are in charge of theirs. It is important to be compassionate and supportive of others, and be giving in ways that they ask.

It isn't my job to ensure another person's happiness, however. Each of us is the only one who can make ourselves happy.

Others are responsible for their happiness

Logrono Rioja: Vegetrian's Heaven
Photo: Miran Rijavec

It is common for pilgrims to leave their walking sticks and shoes near the door in an albergue.

Photo: Miran Rijavec

Traveler as Guest

The number of pilgrims who enjoy the trail has exploded in recent years. Many villages and towns are experiencing unwelcome impacts on their daily lives.

As guests on The Way it is our responsibility to respect the residents who live along the Camino.

Many of the families whose homes, stores, and farms are on the Camino route have lived in their towns for generations but now find themselves as unintended hosts to thousands of people each day.

Being a courteous guest will preserve the welcome reception that pilgrims receive each year.

Be respectful of others' requests

When people ask us not to poop or leave trash in their town, we shouldn't poop or leave trash in their town. It's just the right thing to do.

Photo: Christopher Nowland

Not all thoughts need to be shared

It can be tempting to think that our every thought is brilliant.

When sharing a café table with a couple, one of them asked my husband why he was on the Camino. Before he could answer, she added, "to lose weight?"

No, he replied, he was walking to take time for contemplation and prayer.

I was taken aback but Mark was unphased. He thought that perhaps this woman's comment would have been culturally appropriate in her country. I considered that possibility but still reflected that not every thought that comes to mind must be shared. It is important to consider one's audience and the context of the situation.

I had a similar reaction to the graffiti that can be found on a variety of surfaces along The Way, including people's homes.

We found this graffiti (pictured, left) on the side of a house in Rúa. I doubt that the author would graffiti his own house. Why, then, would the graffiti the side of another's? Messages like these are better written in a card than on walls.

The graffiti on the side of this house reads: "Jill, before we are finished I'd just like to say every step has been better with you. I love you."

Photo: Author

Learn others' languages

Being a native English speaker is both a benefit and a drawback. Many people in other countries learn to speak English in school, so it is common to be able to travel and rely on English and not be forced to learn additional languages. Language is an important element of people's cultures, however, and not being able to communicate in their language limits the amount we can understand about their lives and culture.

Inability to speak or understand your host's language is difficult for other reasons. There were times that Mark and I wandered around towns after misunderstanding directions that had been provided by a local resident. I often got the wrong type of coffee for Mark, although he gratefully drank whatever I brought him.

If only to be sure that you can order a coffee without frustrating both the shopkeeper and yourself, learn at least the basics of others' languages.

Be polite

I live in an environment where it is commonplace, perhaps sometimes expected, that people who encounter one another smile and say a quick, "hi."

Whether people are in the habit of greeting one another or not is not an indication of their warmth or caring. There is a multitude of cultural practices for greetings around the world and it can be difficult to know what is expected.

Greeting everyone you encounter with a smile and greeting isn't a cultural expectation for residents of Northern Spain, however I never met anyone who didn't return my smile.

> Constant kindness can accomplish much. As the sun makes ice melt, kindness causes misunderstanding, mistrust, and hostility to evaporate.
>
> Albert Schweitzer

Top: Catedral de Leon, Photo: Jose Luis Cernadas Iglesias; Photo, right: Author; Photo, bottom: _The Real McCoy

Keep the peace

Medieval villages along The Way typically have narrow streets that can amplify sound.

Particularly in summer, residents sleep with bedroom windows open. Voices of excited peregrinos carry in the early morning when not everyone is ready to rise.

I can be both excitable and loud, a terrible combination for Camino residents in a Medieval village as the sun rises. I had to remind myself that not everyone welcomes my enthusiasm in the early hours, particularly when it rouses them from sleep.

Caminho Portugés; Photo: Artis Rams
Opposite, chapel pews; Photo: neil cummings

Learn others' customs

I spend a lot of time in coffee shops when I am at home. In the coffee shops I frequent, it is customary for people to clear their own plates and trash from their table before leaving. This isn't necessarily the case in Northern Spain nor elsewhere around the world.

At many of the bars and cafés on the Camino the person behind the bar would be working with perhaps one or two other people. There would be a line of hungry and thirsty pilgrims and the bartenders would be working very hard.

Inside a café/bar. Photo: Debbie Parsell

Customers often left their tables with lots of plates and trash piled up. One day I thought I would be helpful to the woman behind the bar. Table by table I cleared the cups, plates, and trash. I even picked up some trash off the floor. I didn't speak enough Spanish to explain what I was doing and she didn't speak enough English to understand what I was trying to say, so I used my best charades to explain that I don't think it is polite for people to leave their dishes for the employees to pick up.

Her response was both confused and mixed and I realized that in being well-meaning I had offended her. In picking up after pilgrims I considered inconsiderate, it appeared to her that I was saying that she hadn't done her job well enough and that I had to do it for her.

It can be easy to act in or interpret a situation based on our own cultural perspectives when we won't really understand it until we examine the same situation from another's perspective.

Opposite, top: It's a Dog's Life: Photo: Banxiety Free; Opposite, bottom: This woman, beautiful in a leopard print dress and espadrilles, stopped tilling her land to pose for a photo. Photo: Author

apitulum huius Almae Apostolicae et Metropolitanae Ecclesiae Compostellanae, sigilli Altaris Beati Iacobi Apostoli custos, ut omnibus Fidelibus et Peregrinis ex toto terrarum Orbe, devotionis affectu vel voti causa, ad limina SANCTI IACOBI, Apostoli Nostri, Hispaniarum Patroni et Tutelaris convenientibus, authenticas visitationis litteras expediat, omnibus et singulis praesentes inspecturis, notum facit: Dnam *Carolam Annam Morrison* hoc sacratissimum templum, perfecto Itinere sive pedibus sive equitando post postrema centum milia metrorum, birota vero post ducenta, pietatis causa, devote visitasse. In quorum fidem praesentes litteras, sigillo eiusdem Sanctae Ecclesiae munitas, ei confert.

Datum Compostellae die 29 mensis Maii anno Dni 2016

Segundo L. Pérez López
Decanus S.A.M.E. Cathedralis Compostellanae

Conclusion

I began this book with the story of my chipped scallop shell, a metaphor for my flawed self, and how, over the course of journeying the Camino de Santiago, I became more accepting of both it and myself.

My experiences on the Camino helped me clarify ideas that I have had for decades. After 25 years of a life busy with family, work, and school, my ideas had become entangled which made them difficult to see clearly or use as guidance.

The brass plate across the middle of this stone marker indicates the number of kilometers to Santiago de Compostela.

The blue square on the top has the image of the scallop shell.

Between the two is a yellow arrow indicating the direction of the Camino de Santiago. Photo: Author

Opposite: My Compostela

If traveling the Camino was a vacation for me, it was a vacation from decisions. The basic choices were already made as I woke, dressed, and walked. I used the time and energy that was freed from choice-making for contemplative reflection. I spent much of that time imagining the person I want to be.

I concluded that self-acceptance is a daily process that lives within the chip of my shell. I can allow the flaws that are an essential part of being human to become a source of agitation or a source of peace. I choose peace.

Many of the thoughts I have shared here act like the yellow arrows that guided me on the Camino. These guiding ideas show me the way to being the person I want to be.

When a choice presents itself, my guiding ideas help me see the circumstance or event, my role in it, and my options for responding to it with greater clarity. That clarity provides me to feel degrees of peace, even in challenging situations.

Feelings of peace benefit both me and those around me. I can share my peace with my family and friends, my students and colleagues, as well as those I encounter only briefly.

Losing perspective on a situation or managing it in a way that is inconsistent with my guiding ideas results in feelings of agitation, even in the simplest of situations.

Those feelings of agitation are detrimental to both me and those around me. When I am agitated I can be short tempered or demanding with my family and friends, my students and colleagues, as well as those I encounter only briefly.

God has my best interest at heart. He looks out for me and cares about my well-being. In that context, He presents me with opportunities to guide my life and expects me to make the best choices I can.

I acknowledge and accept that I am not, nor should be, perfect. My guiding ideas allow me to change direction in a way that recognize my strengths and challenges.

> *You have brains in your head. You have feet in your shoes. You can steer yourself in any direction you choose. You're on your own, and you know what you know. And you are the guy who'll decide where to go.*
>
> *Dr. Seuss*

In addition, through the process of forgiving myself, I can be more forgiving of others.

In using my guiding ideas when I am not sure which direction to head, I feel joy and enthusiasm and am a better person for those around me. Each day I remember that I am blessed.

Photo Credits

Thank you again to all of the talented photographers whose licensing allowed me to include their beautiful images in these pages. The copyright on this book only includes the text and my photographs. Photographers sharing their images through Creative Commons licenses retain all rights to their own artwork.

adrigu

- → *Page 35. (path outside Triacastela) https://www.flickr.com/photos/97793800@N00/5146742134. Licensed CC BY 2.0.*

Alberto Cabrera

- → *Page 61. (arrow in grasses). https://www.flickr.com/photos/jacd74/9456006217. Licensed CC BY 2.0.*

Alex Bikfalvi

- → *Page 16. (people walking by vineyards) Camino de Santiago Act IV. https://www.flickr.com/photos/alexbikfalvi/3633165505. Licensed CC BY-SA 2.0.*

Antonio Lana Diaz de Espada

- → *Page 42. Luis y Fede marcan el ritmo del gruppeto. https://www.flickr.com/photos/antoniolana/5761341196. Licensed CC BY 2.0.*

Artis Rams

- → *Page 105. Caminho Portugés. https://www.flickr.com/photos/artis-rams/15142506528. Licensed CC BY-ND 2.0.*

BanxietyFree

→ *Page 31. Moo. https://www.flickr.com/photos/100132280@N02/16218096692. Licensed CC BY 2.0.*

→ *Page 31. Baa. https://www.flickr.com/photos/100132280@N02/16031390198. Licensed CC BY 2.0.*

→ *Page 85. (boots on rocks) https://www.flickr.com/photos/100132280@N02/16032504249. Licensed CC BY 2.0.*

→ *Page 107. It's a Dogs Life. https://www.flickr.com/photos/100132280@N02/16217815012. Licensed CC BY 2.0.*

Barney Schulte

→ *Page 83. Rainbow Outside Pamplona. https://www.flickr.com/photos/nashvillecorps/14334048989. Licensed CC BY-ND 2.0.*

Christopher Nowland

→ *Page 100. No Poop. No Trash.*

Contando Estrelas

→ *Page 52. Puerta Santa de la Catedral de Santiago. https://www.flickr.com/photos/elentir/4298803046. Licensed CC BY-SA 2.0.*

Daniel López García

→ *Page 79. (Botafumeiro) https://www.flickr.com/photos/dntrotamundos/19203443770. Licensed CC BY 2.0.*

David Dennis

→ *Page 93. Galleta Maria. https://www.flickr.com/photos/davidden/244493216. Licensed CC BY-SA 2.0.*

Debbie Parsell

- → *Page 16. (bunk beds)*
- → *Page 21. (pilgrims on horses)*
- → *Page 30. (cow under vine)*
- → *Page 38. (two women walking)*
- → *Page 45. Santiago Tarts*
- → *Page 60. (three arrows)*
- → *Page 61. (sick figure on road) and (arrow and shell)*
- → *Page 70. Santiago de Compostela*
- → *Page 78. Triaboleiros and Botafumeiro*
- → *Page 84. (path with rocks)*
- → *Page 86. (bunks)*
- → *Page 87. (churros and warm chocolate sauce)*
- → *Page 106. (inside a café/bar)*

Don Oberbeck

- → *Cover photo of shell*

Fresco Tours

- → *Page 11. (scallop shell door handle). https://www.flickr.com/photos/frescotours/29482087723. Licensed CC BY 2.0.*
- → *Page 16. (walking in rain) Camino de Santiago 2012. https://www.flickr.com/photos/frescotours/6929190486. Licensed CC BY 2.0.*
- → *Page 30. (snail). https://www.flickr.com/photos/frescotours/27755281922. Licensed CC BY 2.0.*
- → *Page 30. (roosters). https://www.flickr.com/photos/frescotours/29814939160. Licensed CC BY 2.0.*
- → *Page 30. (horse). https://www.flickr.com/photos/frescotours/28503364401. Licensed CC BY 2.0.*

→ Page 60. (arrow on tree). https://www.flickr.com/photos/frescotours/29686046763. Licensed CC BY 2.0.

→ Page 60. (arrow on building). https://www.flickr.com/photos/frescotours/29838190656. Licensed CC BY 2.0.

→ Page 60. (two arrows on stone wall). https://www.flickr.com/photos/frescotours/27070953084. Licensed CC BY 2.0.

→ Page 61. (arrows in vineyard). https://www.flickr.com/photos/frescotours/27074530923. Licensed CC BY 2.0.

→ Page 87. (lunch). https://www.flickr.com/photos/frescotours/27070986754. Licensed CC BY 2.0.

→ Page 88. (pulpo on plate). https://www.flickr.com/photos/frescotours/6162347359. Licensed CC BY 2.0.

→ Page 88. (pulpo sign). https://www.flickr.com/photos/frescotours/28219706252. Licensed CC BY 2.0.

→ Page 88. (man making pulpo). https://www.flickr.com/photos/frescotours/29906904454. Licensed CC BY 2.0.

→ Page 91. (relaxing in the sun). https://www.flickr.com/photos/frescotours/2668039876/in/album-72157606198886121/. Licensed CC BY 2.0.

Instant 2010

→ Page 28. (group walking). https://www.flickr.com/photos/instant2010/19759316890. Licensed CC BY 2.0

→ Page 77. Frómista-Carrión de los Condes. https://www.flickr.com/photos/instant2010/19758025778. Licensed CC BY 2.0.

→ Page 82. De Mansilla de las Mulas a León. https://www.flickr.com/photos/instant2010/19932156470. Licensed CC BY 2.0.

→ Page 95. https://www.flickr.com/photos/instant2010/9342827655. Licensed CC BY 2.0.

joan

- → *Page 16. (underwear). https://www.flickr.com/photos/minijoan/3647444645. Licensed CC BY 2.0.*
- → *Page 16. (man tending to feet). https://www.flickr.com/photos/minijoan/3781067399. Licensed CC BY 2.0.*
- → *Page 31. (pigs). https://www.flickr.com/photos/minijoan/3651188114. Licensed CC BY 2.0.*
- → *Page 54. (pilgrims reading map). https://www.flickr.com/photos/minijoan/3739097719. Licensed CC BY 2.0.*
- → *Page 61. (Buen Camino). https://www.flickr.com/photos/minijoan/3686949393. Licensed CC BY 2.0.*
- → *Page 92. camino from Santiago to Finistere. https://www.flickr.com/photos/minijoan/3810149911. Licensed CC BY 2.0.*

Jose Antonio Gil Martinez

- → *Page 9. Camino de Santiago. https://www.flickr.com/photos/freecat/2671926522. Licensed CC BY 2.0.*
- → *Page 16. (two women with backpacks) Camino de Santiago - Camino Portugués. https://www.flickr.com/photos/freecat/2845757021. Licensed CC BY 2.0.*
- → *Page 84. (large bricks). https://www.flickr.com/photos/freecat/2845750385. Licensed CC BY 2.0.*

Jose Luis Cernadas Iglesias

- → *Page 33. Catedral de Leon. https://www.flickr.com/photos/jlcernadas/16625183504. Licensed CC BY 2.0.*
- → *Page 56. Catedral de Leon. https://www.flickr.com/photos/jlcernadas/16571443523. Licensed CC BY 2.0.*
- → *Page 103. Catedral de Leon. https://www.flickr.com/photos/jlcernadas/17237407841. Licensed CC BY 2.0.*

Jose Luis Orihuela

→ *Page 54. Camino de Santiago: Alto de El Perdón. https://www.flickr.com/photos/ecuaderno/14362173569. Licensed CC BY 2.0.*

kozumel

→ *Page 93. Savings Time. https://www.flickr.com/photos/kozumel/2160201272. Licensed CC BY-ND 2.0.*

Manel

→ *Page 87. Estrella Galicia. https://www.flickr.com/photos/manel/15234688271. Licensed CC BY-ND 2.0.*

Mark Morrison

→ *Page 67. Waiting for Ann.*

→ *Page 69. Walking with Ann.*

Maria Negrette Photography

→ *Back cover photo of author*

Marta Velasco

→ *Page 30. (dog, top right). https://www.flickr.com/photos/martavel7/18760362202. Licensed CC BY-ND 2.0.*

Miguel Ángel García

- *Page v. St. Jean Pied de Port. https://www.flickr.com/photos/respenda/5808110242. Licensed CC BY 2.0.*
- *Page 36. St. Jean Pied de Port. https://www.flickr.com/photos/respenda/5805492180. Licensed CC BY 2.0.*
- *Page 37. St. Jean Pied de Port. https://www.flickr.com/photos/respenda/5808098522. Licensed CC BY 2.0.*
- *Page 44. Fachadas. Pamplona - Iruña. https://www.flickr.com/photos/respenda/5841594831. Licensed CC BY 2.0.*
- *Page 71. Camino de Santiago 128. https://www.flickr.com/photos/respenda/5822378962. Licensed CC BY 2.0.*
- *Page 73. Vidrieras de la Capilla de San Agustin. Roncesvalles. Navarra. https://www.flickr.com/photos/respenda/5812728952. Licensed CC BY 2.0.*
- *Page 94. St. Jean Pied de Port. https://www.flickr.com/photos/respenda/5805304251. Licensed CC BY 2.0.*

Miriam Mezzera

- *Page 40. Finisterre. https://www.flickr.com/photos/ziamimi/9694394236. Licensed CC BY 2.0.*

Miran Rijavec

- *Page 31. (ducks). https://www.flickr.com/photos/miran/209368183. Licensed CC BY 2.0.*
- *Page 97. Camino de Santiago: Logroño Rioja: Vegetarian's Heaven. https://www.flickr.com/photos/miran/208931819. Licensed CC BY 2.0.*
- *Page 98. Camino de Santiago: Granon Rioja. https://www.flickr.com/photos/miran/208958263. Licensed CC BY 2.0.*

Neil Cummings

→ Page 104. Chapel Pews. https://www.flickr.com/photos/chanceprojects/2814330879. Licensed CC BY-SA 2.0.

_The Real McCoy

→ Page 28. (group sitting in circle). https://www.flickr.com/photos/11204000@N00/14141316031. Licensed CC BY 2.0.

→ Page 48. (vast expanse of Camino de Santiago) https://www.flickr.com/photos/11204000@N00/11421811353. Licensed CC BY-SA 2.0.

→ Page 60. (view above the cloud) https://www.flickr.com/photos/11204000@N00/11420985164. Licensed CC BY-SA 2.0.

→ Page 66. (Buen Camino to your awakening) https://www.flickr.com/photos/11204000@N00/14144556965. Licensed CC BY 2.0.

→ Page 81. (Don't stop walking) https://www.flickr.com/photos/11204000@N00/14141172791. Licensed CC B Y2.0.

→ Page 103. (chapel) https://www.flickr.com/photos/11204000@N00/13957949269. Licensed CC BY 2.0.

Author

→ Page vi. Quiet outside Triacastela. https://www.flickr.com/photos/143386713@N06/28074840712. Licensed CC BY-SA 2.0.

→ Page 19. Rio Burbia Villafranca del Bierzo. https://www.flickr.com/photos/143386713@N06/27898153210. Licensed CC BY-SA 2.0.

→ Page 22. Taxi Relief. https://www.flickr.com/photos/143386713@N06/28179151165. Licensed CC BY-SA 2.0.

→ Page 25. Pilgrim pulling his belongings.

→ Page 30. (cat).

→ Page 39. Day 1, The Purge.

→ Page 51. Monastery of San Xulian de Samos. https://www.flickr.com/photos/143386713@N06/28144919686. Licensed CC BY-SA 2.0.

- Page 53. Wavy Fence. https://www.flickr.com/photos/143386713@N06/28179183465. Licensed CC BY-SA 2.0.
- Page 53. Tart and Café. https://www.flickr.com/photos/143386713@N06/28145057586. Licensed CC BY-SA 2.0.
- Page 53. Three Crosses. https://www.flickr.com/photos/143386713@N06/27899473486. Licensed CC BY-SA 2.0.
- Page 55. Chris and Cerveza.
- Page 58. O Cebreiro. https://www.flickr.com/photos/143386713@N06/27563580723. Licensed CC BY-SA 2.0.
- Page 59. Albergue Casa Domingo, Palas de Rei. https://www.flickr.com/photos/143386713@N06/27563464454. Licensed CC BY-SA 2.0.
- Page 61. (Gallecia sign).
- Page 61. (town signposts).
- Page 64. Faith.
- Page 74. Climb to O Cebreiro. https://www.flickr.com/photos/143386713@N06/27563398764. Licensed CC BY-SA 2.0.
- Page 80. Finding Our Way.
- Page 86. Peregrina Delight. https://www.flickr.com/photos/143386713@N06/27897777180. Licensed CC BY-SA 2.0.
- Page 90. Iglesia de Santiago, Boente, Spain. https://www.flickr.com/photos/143386713@N06/28144820436. Licensed CC BY-SA 2.0.
- Page 84. (small bricks).
- Page 84. (mud path).
- Page 96. Birds in Quiet. https://www.flickr.com/photos/143386713@N06/28100878231. Licensed CC BY-SA 2.0.
- Page 101. Graffiti.
- Page 103. (dog sleeping).
- Page 105. Woman in Leopard Print.
- Page 110. Kilometer marker.

www.ingramcontent.com/pod-product-compliance
Lightning Source LLC
Chambersburg PA
CBHW042058290426
44113CB00001B/12